T0248271

with
love,
grief
and
fury

Also by Salena Godden

Springfield Road: A Poet's Childhood Revisited
Canongate, 2024

Pessimism Is for Lightweights
— 30 Pieces of Courage and Resistance
Rough Trade Books, 2023

Mrs Death Misses Death
Canongate, 2021

Pessimism Is for Lightweights
— 13 Pieces of Courage and Resistance
Rough Trade Books, 2018

LIVEwire
Nymphs and Thugs, 2016

Springfield Road
Unbound, 2014

Fishing in the Aftermath: Poems 1994–2014
Burning Eye Books, 2014

Under The Pier
Nasty Little Press, 2011

with love, grief and fury

Salena Godden

CANONGATE

First published in Great Britain, the USA and Canada
in 2024 by Canongate Books Ltd,
14 High Street, Edinburgh EH1 1TE

Distributed in the USA by Publishers Group West
and in Canada by Publishers Group Canada

canongate.co.uk

1

British Library Cataloguing-in-Publication Data
A catalogue record for this book is available on
request from the British Library

ISBN 978 1 80530 351 0

Typeset in Centaur MT by
Palimpsest Book Production Ltd, Falkirk, Stirlingshire
Printed and bound in Great Britain
by CPI Group (UK) Ltd, Croydon CR0 4YY

This is for the poets and provocateurs, artists and activists, witches and warriors, rebels and raconteurs, full-moon lovers and star sailors, bold-hearts and visionaries, dancers and divas, dawn-drinkers and deep-thinkers, peacekeepers and good-trouble makers, word-weavers and storytellers, prophets and preachers, healers and hope-punks, soul-seekers and big-dreamers.

With Love, Grief and Fury,
Salena Godden

Contents

With Love, Grief and Fury 1   1

Poppies   2

When You Stub Your Toe   5

Tell Good People Good Things   6

Shadow   7

And You Will Go   10

Wish You Were Here   15

The Girl in the Green Cardigan   19

Sweet Cherry Red   23

So Cancerian   30

Seizure   32

Oh, Abundance   33

My Heart Is a Boat   34

Lock   39

Memoirs of Bed Island   44

Happy Birthday Poem   46

From the Mouths of Babes   48

But First Make Tea   49

Bit on the Side   51

Selenophilia   55

1999   56

Hark at You!   59

Cathedrals   61

With Love, Grief and Fury 2   63

Monsters in Autumn   64

Autumn's Secretary   67

Camden   69

Laughing by the Toaster   72

Book Mother   75

Dog Days Done   77

Sorry   79

Do Not Mistake This Smile   83

October Tape Experiment   84

If We Listen to the Ferocious Child and All That   89
    Ferocious Love and Love the Child Ferociously

Grandmother   90

Burned   91

Egg and Spoon Race   97

So, Can You Tell Me About Your Creative Process?   99

4 a.m. Writing Club   100

This Virus   102

All You Have to Do Is Care   103

A Child Washes Up on the Beach   107

With Love, Grief and Fury 3   108

Blackbird   109

We Will Write Poems About You When   111
   You Are Dead

Our Anarchy   113

Bees   114

You Used to Know All the Numbers Off by Heart   117

You Made a Fuss   119

The Then and the Now   122

Evergreen Tea   128

Five Words   138

I Will Walk You Home   142

Notes on Exit and Extraction   143

With Love, Grief and Fury 4   149

Monsters in Spring   151

I Want to Be Your Wife   154

Sun Cream in February   157

Brown Sugar   160

Umbilical   161

Even After the Storm   164

Patient Creature   168

Dirty Old Men   172

One Hundred and Nine   175

Swans Are Hustlers   177

Malasana   178

Sakura   183

Kimono   186

City of Water   191

And the Moon Don't Talk to Me Anymore   193

Cake   197

First Mother   201

A Small Kindness   204

Great-Granddaughters   205

I Cannot Wait to Breathe   206

Your Fears Are Not Prophecies   208

2084   209

Wonderful World   218

Dry Land   219

With Love, Grief and Fury 5   223

Acknowledgements   224

With love and thanks to   226

Last Words   227

With Love, Grief and Fury 1

Summer 2019

Today Iceland held a funeral
to mourn its first glacier
lost to climate change

the Amazon is on fire
and the black smoke
can be seen from space

the global protests
the world is in flame
everywhere, chaos, conflict

I cannot read this page
my eyes blurred with tears
with love, grief and fury

Poppies

The day my first
poetry book was published
it wasn't how I thought it would be.

I was alone in my backyard,
I filled a pot with mud
and planted poppy seeds.

Poking the dirt with my fingers,
I made holes in the earth and
mud caked under my nails.

I knew the poppies
would be beautiful one day –
they would take time to grow,

but what pleasure it would be
to see the first green shoots
and then the first flower bloom.

The day my first
poetry book was published
it was a hot July afternoon.

The air was summer-soft
and the bees were humming
and so I decided I should celebrate.

I went indoors to make a piña colada.
I assembled ice and rum and
pineapple and coconut cream;

I felt so happy in that moment,
but then the blender exploded
splashes of coconut concoction

all sticky all over the kitchen,
up the walls, puddling the floor.
The kitchen was a total mess

but once it was cleaned up
the second attempt worked
that piña colada tasted of

tropical holidays and good times.
I sipped the rum cocktail
and sat alone in the yard,

quietly watching the patch of
still-wet mud and quiet earth,
and I daydreamed about the poppies –

the activity beneath the surface,
the potential and the promise,
how those poppies might bloom one day.

The day my first
poetry book was published
it wasn't how I thought it would be.

I was already grown
and forty years old,
and I felt tired

and like I'd been waiting
such a long time to do this small thing –
to hold a published book in my hands.

I sat alone drinking a piña colada
and I planted poppy seeds,
and then I said cheers to me,

I made a lot of mess
just to sit
here.

When You Stub Your Toe

it hurts you, and in that moment you don't think
of all toes throughout history that hurt. You do
not want to look at other people's stubbed toes.
You do not want to know about people who
have also stubbed a toe. Your pain is now and
here in the present moment. No. You do not
want to read a poem about a toenail moon right
now. No. You do not want to hear a song about
a man who sucked his own toes. Thank you. You
do not want to watch a documentary about
reflexology. No, you do not want a foot massage.
Thank you. No. You do not want to hear a
podcast about chiropody. Your own toe is throb-
bing and it is all you can think about right now.
No human has ever felt a pain like this pain that
is your pain and you have to live with it and live
through it right now and in this moment. I am
sorry. Nobody can do all that hurting for you,
that pain is yours. When you stub your toe it
hurts you, and just you, and in that moment in
time it is just you and your toe.

And so it is with grief.

Tell Good People Good Things

Tell each other you love each other.
Say love. Show your love. Speak it.

Do not wait to talk to a flower
in the hope the dead will hear the love
you could've said before.

Do not wait to talk to headstones
and weep at faded photographs.

Please do not die with all unsaid
and then haunt your loved ones
appearing in night and shadow and dream.

You are alive now. So love now.

Tell your good people all the good things.
Tell each other you love each other.

Do not wait to softly weep to flickering candles
or cry about your love to a flower too late.

Say love. Show your love. Share it.

Shadow

We finish doing a show and we're having a photograph taken outside and I take off my mask to use a smile I prepared earlier and it is hot and summer and so lovely and sunny and I grin for the photograph whilst I think how strange that this photo will be shared in a future when this will be behind us perhaps when scary times have passed and we don't have to wear masks and I am there and I am smiling like it is all alright and like I am in the middle of some summer happy times with the warm sunshine on my face but then I get told off for being big in the centre of the frame and they tell me to move to the side a bit and so I stop grinning and move to the left and shrink to the edge of the group photograph and slip into the dark and I feel dead awkward and apologetic and wherever that photograph is now I know that I shrink and I know I couldn't have hid it as my face betrays all these emotions just as a cloud covers the sun and that image will be evidence of the times and of that day and how I was really shrinking and feeling bad deep down and it will remind me of feeling alone and sad and it will remind me of what hard work it is to appear OK on the surface when your world is on fire and things feel desperately frightening and we're pretending we are fine and if I ever see that photograph it will remind me of that feeling of trying to hide hurt and fear and how anxious and how fragile I can be and how I notice I hold my own hand when I feel anxious and how the left hand holds the right and how the left hand holds the right too tight and after the photo is taken and after I say goodbye and thank you very much and thank you and thank you and bye-bye and I walk the streets of London towards the Marylebone hospital and I'm feeling like I am a shadow and hot and strange and sad and the world is too fast and loud and the people walking past with faces in their masks all sinister and I go to the hospital to see you there in pain and exhausted and battling a monster with your grey and sticky skin and we talk about the weather and hospital food *it's not that bad really* you say *the nurses are so kind* and you're excited to have an ice-cold fizzy orange because your throat and nose are sore with all the tubes and then you ask how the job went and suddenly none of it matters and I laugh and tell you about that awkward group photo which doesn't matter anymore and then we squeeze hands and then I have to just leave you there and you tell me to be brave but that I have to go and you briefly pull your mask down and show me your courageous face and I see how strong you are being and I ask you to promise me that you will be good for the doctors and nurses and do as you are told and rest and you say you will and that you will phone me at bedtime and then I have to go and just leave you there and I leave you and I don't want to leave you and I go and I cry into my mask and I know nobody can see me crying because I have learned how masks are really good for hiding tears and I cry openly with a blue mask covering my feelings as I walk from Marylebone to Oxford Circus like my feet are lead and rocks and the world is hot and loud and busy and sweaty and viral and contagious and terrible and I sit on a busy train with my teary and wet and snotty mask and my left hand holds my right too tight my left hand holds the right and I'm wishing you were here holding hands with me with joy and summer light and then when I am at our front door I put the key in the lock and out of habit I call out *hello* but our house is all hollow and dark and the world too big without you and I'm falling into nothing and this feeling is as scary as hell but someday we'll see how this was and one day you will come home to me and this fear will be a faded history and the sickness will be past and it will all be OK and maybe then one day we will see how I stand awkwardly in this one photograph of this time and see how I hold my own hand and how the left hand holds the right and how the left hand holds the right too tight and see how I fill with lightning with my shadow burning in the sun.

And You Will Go

to new places
that feel as though
they're familiar
and you will go
walk in footsteps
known by ancestors
and your elders
and you will go
to ancient places
and long
forgotten
histories
and you will go
make your own song
build your own fire
and share
your warmth
and you will go
to some soft shore
but be different
every visit
a little older
seashells in your pocket
walking with love

across the sand
and you will go
to the most
difficult place
but each time
a little stronger
every time
letting go
and you will go
and face
the strange
and the cold
and the dark
and you will be
so awfully brave
about it and
we will be so
proud of you
and you will go
and surprise yourself
because it isn't
as easy as it looks
and you will go
dancing, dancing
among the glad
and the joyful
and know it is
blessed and feel
free and happy

and alive in it
and you will go
to the broken place
with the locked door and
the peeling paint
but hold your head up
and know deep down
you have to turn the key
and let your light
flood inside
and you will go
to gardens where
you ought not be
where you are told
you do not belong
and you will go
up to the fancy place
and speak your piece
your hands might shake
but your voice will boom
and you will go
and hold your own
and introduce yourself
you say your own name
take it back from
their mouth and
pronounce it
just as your
grandmothers did

and you will go
and stretch out
your trusting hand
and they will shake it
they will shake your hand
and then you will ask yourself
can they mean me
for surely not
and with that
you will laugh
and you will cry
with your love
grief and fury
you will go
and you will go
and you will go
and you keep going
for you have
many places to be
many faces to see
so much living
to hold in one life
and you will grow
and you will go
and smile your smile
and every time
you will say wow
always, wow
I never felt

like this before
wow, I never ever
felt like this before
oh, my darling
you will say that
every time
and you will go
you will go
you will go
and that's you
you see
you just
keep going
keep going
keep going
keep going
my darling
you will go
go, go, go
and that's what
they will always
remember
and love
about you.

Wish You Were Here

Wish you were here
heatwave. this island is hot. too hot too hot too hot. fam-
ilies get into sticky cars queue on motorways. visit service
stations. share germ and virus. cough cough cough. they
piss and smoke and eat meat pies. suck coffee through plastic
straws that end up in the guts of whales. choking turtles.
suffocating seahorses

Wish you were here
another washed up dinghy. humans flee war and famine and
extreme weather. climate disasters. see how they drown. left
to sink on purpose or taken away to be detained in filthy
cells. no welcome is no welcome. the seaside stinks of it.
the same sea water they fish and trawl is the same soft green
tide they frolic and play in. all laughter. all swimming. all
paddling. splashing in death

Wish you were here
the memory of water. how water remembers everything it
touches and tastes. it is as eternal as space. salt water holds
us in her memory. you weep and mourn. you scatter ashes.
you become mulch for bottom feeders

Wish you were here
the death toll rises. traffic belching fumes. the thick and muggy air. tourists crowding every seaside town. with ripe breath. rough city manners. hear them bark on phones. *well, kids deserve a break.* they say *we need a bit of sea air* as they swarm the beaches. flabby red walrus in musk. elephant seals. mating ritual. during a global pandemic

Wish you were here
record breaking heatwave. the sun burns the skin. beetroot red. raw tuna pink. Cancer laughs his head off sitting on the hot sand with his new pal. see Coronavirus laugh. see Cancer laugh. they are best friends this summer. see them kick a beach ball. watch them play. they share fags in the midday sun. with a persistent cough

Wish you were here
I'm not racist but . . . I want to get black. grill the legs. cook your face. coconut oil. slather it on. sizzling sweat. snake flaking skin. suck a fag and throw the butt. chuck away the empty beer can with the other pretty litter. chew on grease and sugar. lick frozen cow tit milk. piss in the sea. piss in a doorway. piss in a phone box where the defibrillator goes. heart attack and chips. sticks of rock and shit. forget to wash your hands. kiss me quick. spread the virus. *ouch my sunburn hurts ouch*

Wish you were here
see the sun set. a bloody sky. all hell fire. thousands lost.
dead are the refugees. dead are the elderly. dead is the nurse.
dead is the toilet cleaner. dead is the pint puller. dead is
the chippy. all dead now. and so who will wash up? who
will clean the bogs? *sorry* they say *she is not coming into work
today* they say *sorry we tested positive sorry* they say *he got taken
away and never came back.* I forgot to wash my hands of this.
dead are the dead are the dead

Wish you were here
the virus spikes. the death toll escalates. the heat escalates.
the panic escalates. the vulnerable are dying. it is as if the
entire world is suicidal. or that they are in fact murderous.
the sky is spilt red wine. the sea is a bloody graveyard. time
to stay home. stay safe. the screaming child. hot and tired.
stamping on a sandcastle. the entire country is having a
tantrum. so come on then. give it an ice lolly to shut it up.
give it a nice cream tea. give it a battered sausage. give it a
knicker-bocker-glory. knees up mother brown. let the germs
spread. let the lies spread. let the fear spread. drunk wasps
circle overflowing bins. mad seagulls peck at chicken bones.
mounds of trash. beer cans and bottles. smashed glass. over-
flow of raw sewage. flakes of burnt skin and fag ash. plastic
particles and shit. all ingrained into the sand. the pretty
picnic litter. shimmering in the sun. more shit to choke the
sea. a popped plastic beach ball left to strangle birds. garbage
tied tight about the throat.

highest temperatures ever recorded. highest death rates. Cancer and Covid dance. disease and death. Cancer and Covid laugh together. partying. in a heatwave. in a pandemic. in the 2020s

Wish you were here?

The Girl in the Green Cardigan

We are walking
in a long line
in flooded lands —
dirty water, disembogue.
Black mud sloshes underfoot;
traffic, people, sludge, dogs,
a slow trudging and pulling
of suitcases and boxes,
all you can carry —
your life on your back.

A little girl in a green cardigan
looks back to wave to me.
We wave to each other,
we are waving goodbye.
I wave until I can
no longer see her,
until she is a shape
in a paper chain,
silhouetted as
paper elephants
trunk to tail,
pale sun setting
behind them.

I'm alone in all of this,
everything gone,
everyone is lost,
no telling who survived
or where my people are.
I feel it vividly
with pain and sorrow,
the heaviest grief.

I saw another wave —
a monumental monster
crushing everything,
as heavy as a mountain,
angry as all weather.
We knew it was coming
and could do nothing.
You cannot stop water
being water or
people being
people.

Wheels get stuck in thick clag,
splattering oily-brown slurps,
cars and buses and trucks
left abandoned or overloaded
with wet faces squashed
against bloody smashed glass.
I have no choice but to
follow the crowds on foot,

perhaps to higher ground and safety,
but all is catastrophe and chaos.

The smell of human fear and stink
and smoke and burning debris;
people begging, pushing and shoving,
turning ugly, stealing and fighting
each other, and every person wishing
for these times before times:
when home was a nice home,
when home was safe and still,
when there was once a cool pillow,
and when that was once
our own safe bed in a room
in a home where love sleeps.

But it is all lost and rubble
under silt and water.
No bed, no home, no love,
nothing and nowhere,
we are lost, dispossessed.

Some seem prepared –
I have an envy for
good sturdy boots and coats,
batteries and tinned food,
torches and tools and tents.

I jealously watch people find people,
how they weep and hold each other.

Then under a bent tree
I observe two boys with a phone.
They are out of their heads,
mad and bitterly laughing,
cackling, sitting in the mud,
reading social media posts out aloud,
the last goodbyes we shared.

I am shivering.
I look down at my own
trembling filthy hands,
in which I appear to hold
a crumpled photograph
of the little girl
in the green cardigan.
She is sitting on a bicycle
and squinting in the sun.

Sweet Cherry Red

sweet
cherry red
crop top

tiny red cherries
each button is sweet
red cherries in pairs
against her soft
brown breasts

sweet
cherry red
crop top

from
TopShop
the faded blue
ripped denim
wet-look curls
piled high
and legs long
as summer

sweet
cherry red
crop top

how anytime
man wanted
man could yank
a branch down
pull cherries
off a tree with
grabbing fists
chew them up
spit the pits
man tramples
on cherry blossom
stamps on petals
with filthy
farm boots

sweet
cherry red
crop top

sweet sixteen
sweet brown girl
picture her
at a cottage
down a track
wild cornflowers

on the edge of
nothing for miles
nobody to know

hear the music
the needle
going around
listening to
Crosby, Stills,
Nash & Young
on vinyl
helpless, helpless
blue skies and
silver smoke
and cold beers
flies circling
flies landing in
mash banana
gone brown

sweet
cherry red
crop top

feeding
three babies
one, two
and three
white hair and

pink faces covered
in snot and want
crawling in bonfire ash
and hay-yellow grass
see the yard
the axe and
the log pile
splinter and glass
rope and beer tins
ants and bees
a jam-covered toy car
that sweet smell of
nappies and mayhem
warm milk and incense
hashish and woodsmoke

one man has the
bonnet open on the truck
head in the engine
comes up for a smoke
stops to drink
his home brew
from a jam jar
oily hand and
black fingernails

sweet
cherry red
crop top

sits on a log
sucking on a
liquorice roll-up
whilst playing with
the three babies
she reads a story
does the voices
sings the youngest
softly to sleep

man wipes
his oily dipstick
the other man
chops wood
chop-chop
man stops
and says
she has
pretty hair
man looks over
and laughs
and says
yeah she does
man grins filthy
lovely curls
man laughs
imagine that hair
tickling your belly
man and man

laughing a dirty
man laugh

sweet
cherry red
crop top

is retreated
she is budding
inside there
and she is a pip
she is as cherry flesh
she is as sweet juice
she is as blossom
she is a whole damn
cherry orchard
but she don't know

man chops
dry wood
cherry tree
burns good
the roaring fire
the burning sun
heat and smoke

sweet
cherry red
crop top

sweet sticky baby
boy on the lap
sucking milk
from a bottle
tiny baby
sleeping sound
in a pram
but the third baby
she's all naked
and barefoot
tottering about
the ramshackle yard
sucking a lighter
toddling backwards
towards the fire

So Cancerian

'What can I say it is my birthday and yes I guess I have been so Cancerian lately so crabby-pants and so jumping June bugs and so midsummer's baby and so summer solstice magic and yeah and wow look at me all dancing sideways across wet sand like a sassy sexy crab and how I wanna retreat into this cold rockpool and smoke and cry about the sea and look at the bright stars and so come and watch me dance but no don't look how pretty I am right now failing to respond because this world hurts and it is a bit ouchy out there and fast and I wanna climb into my shell and hide and live inside a piano like a tiny happy mouse but hey I feel like you are noticing my shiny-shiny shell and so come on then looky-look how I spin gold and I can juggle my eyes and annoy even myself then how I want to run away to an island and live on coconuts and hug you and thank you and love you and then I want to pinch you and go skirling off skittish sideways and act weird because it was weird or I was always weird and both but come on let's get really drunk and cut our own fringe and burn the hair and then mark our faces with ash and strip naked and sing hallelujah to the night and oh now it got weird again but I can make a quick toastie if you are hungry are you hungry want some of this stew it took two centuries to make and no bother at all it's no bother take it and take my right arm I hate having two arms one is enough for me and I don't mean to be rude but I really want to lick the salt off your skin and look into your beautiful eyes where I can see your ancestors and wow now I am thinking how like gravity freaks me out I mean why don't we just fall off the earth and I think I need more water and more time to think and walk and you know I get so lost just thinking about all the feelings I feel in this present moment and in this one lifetime and sorry but life is so short and death is a real thing that happens oh sorry I made it weird again and ooh look at the beautiful full moon'.

Seizure

As my sister eats ice cream with me
she is struck by lightening
thunder cracks and rolls through her
her hands like eagles' claws to grab the sky
as she cries and hurtles far away
her eyes fixed on gods that seize her
their fire reflected in her black pupils
her body ridged and convulsing
her breath faltering, stuttered
nothing I can do but hold her
and tell her I love her and
ask her to come back to me
violence and vulnerability
ice cream goes everywhere
her head is on my shoulder
I stroke her soft black hair
as the last rumbles echo
and as the storm passes
she tells me she loves me too
grinning face messy with weather.

Oh, Abundance

Give more, yes, we know, it will never be enough, but give more, give of yourself, give your time, give your energy, your magic, your joy, your tears, give until it aches in your chest, yes, we know, it will never seem to be enough, but it is in the act of the giving you shall know abundance, so give more, be more generous, give back more, yes, we know, it will never seem to be enough, but just when you think you have nothing left to give, you may find you can give more, so give more, give your heart, give your light, and no, sorry, it will never seem to be enough, not really, not in just one lifetime, but try and give more, give more, give back, and be thankful, and say *thank you*, and pay it forward, and share more and give more, and love more, for it is in this state of giving you live, oh, abundance, we see you alive in there, you are a river of flowers, overflowing with colours and riches that can never be counted in coin.

My Heart Is a Boat

We're outside a pub
and she's yelling,
telling me to,
Get back on my boat

My friends say, *she's just racist,*
but I put down my rum
and walk over and ask,
Do you need a hug?

I stand with open arms
as wide as a map of the world,
and she bursts into tears.
I hold her for a while.

My jacket gets stained
with orange foundation,
my lapels are streaked
with black mascara.

The pub is rumbling
under the mad full moon
and the spring tide
crashes to shore.

My heart is a boat —
my ancestors' longships,
my grandmother's Windrush,
the rubber dinghies sunk without trace.

My heart is a boat —
my ancestors' longships,
my grandmother's Windrush,
the rubber dinghies sunk without trace.

Vast ocean and destiny,
the horizon, the sea,
home in my bones
forever singing to me.

The unknown ahead,
the unseen and untold
ancients, old souls
their stories unfold,

ancestors' spirit
holding them dear,
ghosts of the elders —
history lives here,

the truth under water,
the thin paper words:
Welcome to Britain
cold and unheard.

And who's left behind?
And what did you leave?
Shivering at Tilbury Dock
your young hope and belief

come willing, come able,
your mother country calls
to help the war effort
to build road and walls.

Hale and hearty
immigrant sons
sent to the frontline,
trench foot and guns

and taking a bullet,
march side by side
for country and crown,
for honour, for pride,

singing 'Jerusalem'
This green and pleasant land
give with whole heart,
Queen waves with gloved hand.

Movement of people
the tall tales told
invited to London
the streets paved with gold

We bring the music,
culture, colour, spice,
trading the sunshine
for rain, snow and ice,

trading the peoples,
sugar canes, daughter,
if Kingston is my pepper
then London saltwater

and rivers of tears
that stick in the throat.
We sail to the truth –
my heart is a boat.

We dream of the heat,
the warmth of home,
we dream of the soil
where our roots were grown.

My heart is a boat
and I sail through time.
My boat has a heart,
we share the bloodline.

Our heart is a boat,
our boat is a heart
keeping us united
when we're torn apart.

See the ocean at night,
stars shifting above
mirrored in moonlight
reflecting ONE LOVE.

The seabed is a cemetery,
nameless, timeless, space,
seawater holding memories
of past, person and place.

Our boat is a heart
and love is for free —
welcome aboard
us, them and we.

My heart is a boat
My boat is a heart
My heart is a boat
My boat is a heart.

Lock

You knock and bang on the windows, but cannot remember how to get in or out. The first time it happens you are thrown spinning through the air and then are on your knees in the road. Dry autumn leaves under the palms of your bleeding hands. Minutes leading up to the event are erased. The moment scratched out. You were flown and flung through the air and into the gutter.

Another time, it is so blurry, but a bang to the head, a taste of metal and blood. You see how your lip is bleeding in the mirror of a bathroom. Public bathrooms are the worst. Sometimes, if you daydream, you forget where you are. Then you wash your hands and look into your reflection for a moment, fix your hair, smooth your frown, but then upon returning to the bar there is no recollection of who you were drinking with or where you were sitting or what bar or city or century it is. Stand still. Stand there in the bar, with no memory of it, clammy hands, short breath, heart pounding and wait there. You hope someone will shout your name and you hope that your name brings the present to your present mind. Inside that locked moment, you consider that perhaps you are a figment of your own imagination and you aren't even real or really there. You imagine that you are invisible. You imagine that the whole world is a hallucination. You are like a child lost in a supermarket. This has happened a few times. What happened? Exactly. What happens? Inexplicable.

Another time you are sitting with a friend in a garden in summer, listening and talking, just sitting and talking with a friend in a garden. And suddenly you go and you are gone. You are swirling here and there and above the conversation, the afternoon, the bees in the flowers. Time is erased. Then when you return, you feel bewildered, but dare not ask how long you've been gone. What your face and body did when you were absent. Did the friend notice you were not present? And the birds, yeah, they still sing and the friend, yeah, is still merrily talking, but you are too scared to ask: did you see me go? Did you see where I went? Was I gone a long time that time? Where did I go? I definitely was not here.

You are in a taxi. You daydream, like I said, sometimes it is dangerous to do that, you look at the scenery, the city all buzzing and blurring out of the car window and then suddenly you look down at your hands and at the cab seat and at the back of the driver's neck and panic and cannot remember the destination or why you are alone in a cab. What makes it worse is that you had been in an identical taxi the day before, but this is another cab ride and another day entirely. Heart banging in your chest. You recognise a street and, at a stop sign, open the car door, run from the taxi driver in terror. But you don't live in that area anymore, you momentarily forget where you live, you forget where it is safe, you pull your coat shut and walk across London for miles and hours.

You get locked out of what is and what isn't. Terrorised by stories you tell yourself and what the mind is half-remembering and rewriting. Flashback. Danger. Memory. Alarm. Vibrations. Buzzing in the ears. You touch your face, your own skin, always that familiar creeping feeling, like how did it happen? How did we get here? Where have I woken up this time? Put frozen peas on a black eye. Vague memory of needing to escape, to run from something or someone. Or perhaps suddenly needing to run towards something or someone. From or to? Pushed or jumped? Urgent. Emergency. Face meet pavement. Pavement meet face. You ring a friend.

They tell you that they think you ran into a wall. But it wasn't a wall, surely, it was a door, did you see there was a door there? Can you see the shining windows in all the Soho pavements? And with that the darkness laughs with the familiar voice from a black night so long ago, a treacherous voice in the ear, trapped inside, outside, underneath.

Lock the door and close the curtains. You are barricaded inside and outside. You lock yourself out and keep a darkness in. Easy mistake to make. It is a bit like watching a movie; the actors use your body. Or perhaps like being a puppet with another entity pulling your strings. You are forced to watch the show, whilst yelling at the screen to wake up. And you are just a doll, you fall in slow motion; a fall down the stairs, a shove into a river, a stifled scream into a pillow. A sensation of falling through water, falling through space, falling through a window, falling through the pavement, all of which did or didn't happen. What isn't real makes sense. You feel abandoned, left to stumble, to sink or swim, to wake up bleeding on some rocks. How you run, alarm in the brain, the urgency. It is like smack-ing your own face with a door you slam shut on yourself.

These pavements are treacherous treacle. These windows all paper. The stairs greased with lard. And all the gritty gutters get rubbed across your cheeks. The night is a stuttering film of sky, it is old footage being played in a loop. Keys are lost. World gone slippery and sideways. You are Alice, falling down the holes and between the cracks. Falling, falling, falling, through to the other side, another world, landing outside of yourself, beside your self, locked in or locked out or both.

Memoirs of Bed Island

I mark the passage of time
by counting swallows
making love upon the wing,
and think of you, my dear
and the thing done
difficult and bloody.

I've got library books,
a new notebook and pen,
tea and shortbread,
a view of my
tomato plants
on my window sill.

I fall asleep at 11 p.m.
but wake up at
codeine o'clock.
I must not speak
of it or show
any self-pity.

It is raining,
wind rattling
the windows.

My empty belly,
my blood, my pain,
my nothing,

but we won't dwell
or tell anyone.
Just ride each
awful painful truth,
no time for what
could have been.

It's a mission to get
supplies from the kitchen
to my duvet raft,
my book boat,
the horrors
are real.

I hide my
predicament
alone in here
all summer.
I wait for it to pass,
until I can walk

away from the
bloody mess
we made.

Happy Birthday Poem

And how can it be
that we are just beginning
and not in the middle
but closer to the start
that we hold such hope and faith
when calamity is the bassline
and catastrophe the chorus
that when we wake each morning
we reach not for gun and rum
but pen and heart and time
that the party just got started
like yesterday was a dress rehearsal
thank you, the first one was nice
but the next is always stronger
and we're not even halfway
and healing is our power
forgiveness is an ocean
and shrinking was an error
and dreaming was a gift
and never giving up
how can it be
we care more now and
love more fiercely than ever
when once death was a space

the end a destination
and black was not a dress
and sex was not a passport
but learning always sexy
just look at this tattoo we never had
and look at the geography
all the places we haven't been
the languages unspoken
and all the shoes we never wore
the science and the nature
the doors that we can open
paintings on the eyelids
this love, this life, my love
how we cannot eat it all
but we stuff our face with laughing
and drink in all the summer
and still stay up too late
and how can it be
we're just getting going
learning to dance
to sing our own tune
that this is just beginning
and change is a constant
and how can it be that
there is more to come

From the Mouths of Babes

It's a beautiful June evening.
I'm reading in my garden,
drinking a chilled glass of wine
and listening to summer —
a bee is in the roses,
I hear it buzz and
I can hear my love
in the house, he is
singing in the kitchen,
and chopping chives
to put in a potato salad.
A child plays so happily
in a neighbour's garden,
I hear her voice now
high-pitched and screaming.
Through a hole in the fence
she gaily sings to me,
'Kill yourself. Kill yourself.'

But First Make Tea

Five good morning posts

Good morning – Today is a day they hath named Nowday. Now is a perfect time to step into your future self in present form, but first some long think and many tasks that will test endurance and spirit and mettle, but first make tea.

Good morning – It is another day. Take one day at a time. One page at a time. Try to remember to use more guts stuff and heart stuff not always just the head stuff. Give the overthinks a rest today. The past is here and so is thy future, we meet in the present, but first make tea.

Good morning – For a moment just imagine having a lifetime of sunrises all in the same morning, how intense that would be, you think you want it all, but one sunrise per day is quite enough, do one job well at a time, rise and shine, but first make tea.

Good morning – Waking up hungry in this dark morning of the human, maybe porridge is the answer or justice or spring, probably all three, but first make tea.

Good morning – Time is liquid. Notice how each moment pours into the next. Swim into it. You're made of water and light. Your tides grow strong each day, look at you, you really are as miraculous as a fish, take a deep dive into new waters, but first make tea.

Bit on the Side

You steal time
to write nowadays
feels like a hook-up
in a roadside motel
you sneak a go on
a fancy side piece
right now it feels
so wrong it's write
you slag around
behind the back
of the to-do list
you have these
others in your head
flirting with you
giving you the eye
licking their lips
tempting you with
a curvy line of verse
a hot slut mess
on speed dial
dirty notes
just lying there
naked
and wanting

to meet up
for a quickie scribble
you taste the idea
on the tip of
your tongue
a free-write
splashy outpouring
you're a cheat
you're a thief
stealing hours to write
and grabbing handfuls
of new words
you're up at dawn
and when no one is awake
you tiptoe about
pocketing notebooks
tucking pens up your sleeve
even this very poem
is just a bit on the side
and it feels a bit sexy
and a bit naughty
to write this
forbidden page
see this new poem?
you read it now
this is not on the to-do list
are you seeing this?
it's a sneaky poem
it's a cheeky poem

it is not meant to even exist
you have gone off on one
and it's just you and this page
and you get lost in it
pleasure and pain
and want and need
pressing letters
touching typing
you finger the keys
you love it
lick it
feel it hot
and swirling whirling
writing new worlds
over and over
again and again
clean sheets of
smooth white paper
filthy with feeling
and gush of ink
and thoughts and
reasons and dreams
and people and voices
you've never written before
and it is so fucking exciting
and it is alive and real
alive . . . pulsating
until you stop full stop
crack a window open

smoke a filthy fag
the sun has risen
as you take a shower
make up some excuses
why you spent hours
writing a thing nobody asked for
put your swimming kit on
tell them you are at the pool
tell them that is why
you can't answer the phone
tell them that is why you are wet.

Selenophilia

How I would like to fuck the moon
hot moon rocks nudging skin
sway gently on her moony face
get wet and wide and slide her in
how I would like to fuck the moon
push the moon juice deep in south
in and out and hard and round
until moonlight pours out of my mouth
how I would like to fuck the moon
full and whole and bright is she
riding on the moon all night
from black hole to infinity
how I would like to fuck the moon
gently tease and ease her in
feel the moon, full and whole
burning dreams of her within
how I would like to fuck the moon
taste her wine and milky breast
lick her salt and suck her clit
all night long, without a rest
vibrating on the moonshine face
squirting into stars and space
I'd kiss her, eat her outer space
how I would like to fuck the moon.

1999

We went for karaoke
in the Korean district

like a newborn foal I staggered
hooking arms with Chance

a boy with a name like that
he had to be hedging his bets

he was all teeth and smiles
I have a clear memory of it and how

I wore high-heeled sheepskin boots
a denim mini-skirt, Raspberry Beret

Chance and me in the Korean district
we walk to buy a pack of Lucky Strikes

but outside the 7-Eleven
we find a box of notebooks on a bench

like a baby on a doorstep without a note
or more like all the notes without the baby

vulnerable in a rain
of flashing neon purple

sex shops and bad ideas
the Erotic City of Korean bars

I read something scribbled
about a Lady Cab Driver

and a pizza box that was delivered
with a message written in the lid

we sniff the pages
and touch the paper

wary of hidden cameras or
of being watched by the author

imagine that, all your diaries
just left in the street, abandoned

I picked out one book and I felt sorry
for the lost poems and dreams

the orphaned first lines and all
the forgotten ideas and conclusions

so I put the notebook back
with its brothers and sisters

their covers all covered with
zig-zag biro drawings and doodles

a childlike love heart
with the letter P

written in the middle
P means something to the

the loser of notebooks
love for P and a big love heart

and later when Chance
takes a chance and kisses me

in the elevator on the way back up
to the Korean Karaoke lounge

I keep thinking about the notebooks
we leave on trains and hotel bedside tables

in telephone booths, libraries and pubs
so I dedicate this to the losers of notebooks

and this one is for P
I say: hit number 23

I only want to see you laughing
laughing in the Purple Rain.

Hark at You!

'To be honest I always preferred their early work. They were better when they were angry and raw and edgy. I liked it when they had no confidence and low self-esteem. When their feet were bare and their wounds all bloody and the scars weren't healed. When they had less fancy ideas and more punk spirit. When they didn't know their way home, because they had no home and no way. When they didn't know their own worth. When it was all for free. Yeah. When they were miserable and broken and suicidal. That was the best stuff, you know, when they were skinny and hungry and more grateful. When they'd gaze upon us with wet and shiny eyes, tears in their lashes, and they'd say thank you, thank you, thank you, master and king and god and lord, thank you. And they'd fall at your feet and beg for you to listen and look and how they'd yearn for your feedback and praise as they poured their raw ideas into your ears. Then how they would kiss your ring and be soaked in gratitude and rain and cheap wine piss and glorious effort. Look at the state of them now.

Hark at you! Look at you and your shiny shoes. Look at you with a dress on. Look at you with your arms and legs and eyes and lips. Look at you doing with your own life what you always said you wanted to do with your own life. Hark at you! All high and mighty! I bet you drink water. I bet you are hydrated. I bet you are expecting to be paid for your work and time. I suppose you'll be wanting a taxi home safe too? Cor! Blimey! Taxi? Home? Safe? You've changed! Hark at you!'

Cathedrals

Each morning we build cathedrals. We decorate them with sea shells and eyelash-salt, warm light and dreams of butterflies.

But by nightfall, nothing remains but trampled sandcastles, coppery and tarnished green, a fear of the night that drowns us, then the sea that washes it away.

Each morning we build cathedrals. We decorate them with gold dust and sea-salt kisses, chocolates and silver rings and summer things and dreams of flying flowers.

But by nightfall nothing remains but a stray dog pissing in winter's doorway, a fear of the fear, as the blood of Friday night washes us away.

Each morning we build cathedrals. We decorate them with violet dawn light and dreams of flying, and dreams of dreams of flying.

But by nightfall nothing remains but a list of things to do and a mesh of things unanswered, and the dreadful knowledge that we are not what we intend to do – we are what we already did, intentionally.

And each morning we build cathedrals. This one is made of paper, we decorate it with glitter, phosphorus and ribbons, we ink and hand-print our best intentions, we brush it with milk and prick it with a fork and bake it.

But by dusk, nothing remains but a rusty caravan, empty balloons are ripped condoms, there's the fear of the plump shadow, and the vodka washes all the best wishes down, with the laughter like a drain.

This morning you built a cathedral, you rose, you bloomed with prick, kick and thorns. This one has a thick skin of rubber, it will be stronger this time, as forgiving and elastic as love, love, over and over, again, love, over and over again.

With Love, Grief and Fury 2

Autumn 2045

Well, kid, then there was an escalation of fear and ignorance, chaos and division and war and destruction but back then some people kept quiet because they were worried they'd lose Twitter followers.

What's Twitter, Mama?

Hmm, hard to explain, kid. There was a time when we tried to communicate and share dreams and hopes electronically, but we spent a great many hours arguing semantics and politics and comparing our lives with each other online, and we wrote notes to each other called 'tweets' with these machines we called 'smartphones', and people shared pictures of cats and avocados and fun dance crazes, and sadly most of the time people lied about their lives and exaggerated how happy they really were.

Woah, that sounds crazy, Mama!

I know, kid, I know, now please stop asking so many questions about the twenties and finish your cockroach soup.

Monsters in Autumn

It's the first days of autumn, red leaves and yellow sunshine.

Writing Monster yawns and stretches and makes a pot of tea for Gigging Monster, who has just got home from smashing it at festivals. Writing Monster whispers about the change in light, notices that the nights are drawing in, shows us books and candles and the fluffy bed socks. She says, 'Poor thing! You must be so tired now, you must need to rest. You performed all summer. Stop gigging! Now it is my turn, my time to dance on the page and watch the frost and wintry dawn. I hope you sold some books this summer. I hope you have saved some money so we can eat this winter, I hope you have not spent it all on rum and shiny things!'

Gigging Monster curses and bursts into tears. It is the end of the party. The end of summer. The end of daylight. She hates the end of any thing. She runs upstairs and throws herself on the bed and weeps about her love for poets and parties. She pours on the guilt, boasting about a standing ovation, she wails, 'but I love gigging, performance is a happy place . . .' Gigging Monster is so needy, she demands all of my attention, so much dancing at sunrise around campfires.

Writing Monster has been locked in a box and sleeping all summer, as Gigging Monster toured and raved and collected ideas for stories and songs. Gigging Monster is exhausted and emotional. She pours a shot into her tea, she is smoking fags continually as she whines 'I love to travel, and I like fun and I will miss the laughs'. She tells me she has torn a pocket on the suit and lost my red lipstick down a compost loo.

Writing Monster tells me I stink of bonfire smoke. She gently suggests that I could listen to an audiobook and soak in the bath and comb the bits of grass and twig out of my hair. Writing Monster speaks in soothing tones, she offers me my soft pyjamas and whispers 'Please come back here . . .' as she shows me the new novel we want to finish.

And here I am, stuck in the middle. It is like this every year during the first days of autumn. As soon as the light changes, I am thrown about in this battle, a clash of ego and mania, pull and push, dark and light, summer to winter, the cycle, the conflict of inside and outside, introvert and extravert. There is no rest with my monsters.

Yet it is with wonder that we watch summer end and autumn begin, my monsters and I, we collect the first conkers of the year, every year, we arrange them in a bowl placed in the centre of the kitchen table as though they are the first conkers we have ever seen.

These monsters, these brain bullies, I made them, I feed them, I hold them, I need them, I hate them, I love them, and as the decades pass I am trying to learn to balance them equally.

Autumn's Secretary

I want to be autumn's secretary in soft corduroy and velvet, shades of russet, saffron and auburn. I am burnt caramel, warmed chocolate in a tight toffee skirt and heels.

I am autumn's secretary, my new glasses on my nose, my hair piled high on my head. I knock on her door and bring her a pumpkin spice latte and the morning papers, the headline reads: *Summer Found Dead in Woods.*

I am autumn's secretary: Yes, thank you, Ms Autumn, I nod earnestly, Yes ma'am, I'll get that sent off right away, yes, boss, as I finish taking dictation. On my lunch break I have butternut soup. Then I sit and write the minutes at the board meeting, the accounts team discuss profit and loss, maple leaf fall and wind-blown apples.

I am autumn's secretary. She asks me
to stay and work late, again. This time
she says we have to collect conkers, file
the chestnut account, plus there's a
backlog of truffles, delicious, pungent
and ripe. When she calls me into her
office, she pours me a glass of burgundy.
Her heady smell of rich earth, black-
berry, tree bark, mushroom-butter, I
melt when she touches me, I want her
attentions, a swirl of my favourite
colours on the tip of my tongue.

Camden

Remember the best times of your life when you'd walk from your tiny flat all the way to Camden Market to buy tights and it was three pairs for a fiver and you'd take ages picking the colours and patterns and you'd buy three pairs of tights and feel so rich and so happy because although you wear the same cowboy boots you always wear and the same skirt again and again you'd at least have new tights with no holes for a change and you would feel lighter and how you'd walk happily by Camden Lock with your boot heels clipping on the wet and shining cobbles and you'd see the punks and goths drinking cider by the canal and you'd go into a pub like the Hawley Arms and have a pint of beer and maybe some chips and find that quiet corner to write and you'd be so content with your shopping and so happy with the three pairs of colourful tights for a fiver and maybe you also bought some silver hoop earrings for a quid and a packet of Nag Champa joss sticks from the hippy stall and a butternut squash and a nub of ginger to make a big pot of soup or a curry which would feed you for a few days and you'd write about it all in a new notebook with your blue fountain pen and you'd write the date on the first front page in big curly letters and marvel at how the years are passing and you'd write about how this felt like a happy and special day you would never forget . . .

and that this was really it and you were here and writing and even though you were lost just for once in that small moment you felt found and there was a shift just then because you had made these small purchases for yourself and you lived on your own for the first time and you were living your messy life and writing every day and you hoped you would be better now even though it was a task to remember to eat and sleep and look after yourself and your hair was knotty and your left boot had a piece of cardboard in it to cover the hole in the sole and your life was a fiasco of bad choices but books felt like a safe space and your girlfriend Kelly would text to say she was at Camden Tube station and on her way to meet you and you would feel excited to see her knowing that later you'd probably have another funny Saturday hanging out in Camden and eating truffles from a paper bag and laughing at everything and you might walk down to the Good Mixer like last time and play pool with a young Amy with her cool tattoos and pink ballet shoes and her girlfriend and the four of you girls might play doubles and drink pints and laugh and smoke fags and have a perfect hour or two which means nothing at the time but so much more now as you see how you wrote about it all here in your diary and as you wrote that page you looked down at your pen in your hand and you see how it looks the same as your hand now writing *this* page because your hands haven't changed too much and neither has the memory and so maybe this is your reminder . . .

to please try to remember the lost hours and the nothing days and make space for ordinary glimmers of joy as they could be illuminating some of the best times of your life and you'd not even know until so many years later when you remember walking all the way to Camden Market to buy tights and you'd get three pairs of tights for a fiver and feel so rich and so happy . . .

Laughing by the Toaster

You call my name
from the lounge
and you laugh
that same laugh.

I swear I'll turn
and see you
twenty-five years old,
all blue eyes and smiles,

I'm in the kitchen
and I hear the way
you call my name,
the way only you say it,

I expect you to appear,
plectrum in your teeth,
long dirty blond hair
hanging in your face,

laughing about
some joke or playing
me a song
by Tom Waits,

and I laugh
because
I love your laugh,
it makes me laugh

but when I turn my head
it is a crazy hot second,
because I see you now
suddenly fifty years old

all blue eyes and smiles,
and in that moment
it is amazing to me,
— look at us!

You and me here
in our kitchen,
laughing
by our toaster,

laughing
which makes me
laugh, again,
writing this,

just thinking
about the laughter
and the way we laugh,
and how we are together,

and how you'll
play me a song,
and how the
music is forever,

how time
is an illusion
and nothing
but fast and fleeting

and we are
always here,
you and me and love,
laughing by our toaster.

Book Mother

So, the other day, at a dinner, somebody asked me, 'Do you have children?' and it was OK, I mean, it didn't feel judgemental, it felt like a natural question whilst making small talk about family. However, in answer to the question, I suddenly heard myself blurt, 'I love books,' and then there was a nod and a pause. I waited patiently, just like any mother, to share pictures of books on my phone. The conversation moved on, of course, I didn't show them any photos, but how I longed to tell this person about all these great authors and powerful poets I love; the books that changed my life and the journeys books have taken me on. How I love to write, too, to be inside words. And how books have taken me all over this world and to other worlds. And how hard I have had to push and how very difficult the labour was, how much it hurt and stretched and challenged me, how each book has taken years to birth. And how the book I'm currently nursing is keeping me up every night. I get no sleep. I do not rest. My body aches with it. I know so many beautiful and brilliant writers that manage to have it all, books and babies, but it was not for me: the timing was never right. I have to admit that ship has sailed, but to be fair, I never went to the port on time to board it. I had such little interest in babies, I don't remember ever wanting to make babies nearly as much as I wanted to make books. I wanted to read and write, selfishly and greedily. How it's been a sacrifice, a privilege, a struggle and an honour. Look at my library, see these creations. Ah, look how they are getting big, look how the years are flying by, see how fast they grow. Funny how you forget about the sleepless nights and tantrums, once you hold your own book in your hands.

Dog Days Done

Summer lifts her skirt
revealing a glimmer of

amber, light and yellow.
Summer takes her time

to pack her belongings,
her weary butterflies

and thirsty bees.
And somewhere

in a distant field
August writes

goodbye letters
in gold on hay

and corn and
chestnut and you.

The morning after
the first thunderstorm

you'll open the window
and smell it changed,

wafts of smoke,
and rain and past.

This ending
is a beginning.

Make hay
and make love,

gather bilberries
and blackberries.

Dog days done,
Sirius is south,

the last burst of roses,
apples and cider,

the Lughnasadh feast,
the tomato harvest,

the fruits so red and ripe
in September's hands,

summer feeding
autumn's mouth.

Sorry

I think I said the word sorry over one hundred times in the last three hours?

Sorry, I said. Sorry to the old lady as I walked down the bus aisle and one of my three heavy bags brushed her coat hem and she tutted at me. I said sorry. Sorry to the woman on the bus that said something-something 'buggy' and I heard her and turned and said sorry because I thought I was in the way of her buggy but she wasn't getting off at that stop or talking to me. So then I nodded and said sorry again. Sorry to the whole bus. Sorry I have too many bags and only two hands. And a good handful more apologies mumbled and thrown in there every time someone needed me to move so they could get on or off the bus. Sorry to that same first old lady when she got off at her stop and I was trying to get out of her way, and she elbowed me on purpose. Yes. I just said sorry to her for elbowing me. Sorry to a man sitting next to me on the Tube train, because his elbow touched mine and he needed lots more room to do his phone game thing. I put my phone in my bag and looked at the floor and said sorry.

Sorry to everyone as I was getting on the escalator because I knew I was too slow to get on the escalator, sorry for me and my only two hands and my three heavy bags, and I got confused which hand to hold the rail with and which to hold all three bags. Sorry getting through the Tube ticket barrier again for going too slowly and the girl said no problem and that was nice and I felt weirdly grateful. Thanks I said a few times and not sorry.

Sorry. I quickly rang my mum to say sorry that I was late, I'm on my way but that I'm gonna be about an hour late. Sorry. Got to Waterloo and boarded my train to visit my mum with three heavy bags and found a seat. OK. I then said sorry several times to the man sitting opposite with headphones on because I needed him to stop swamping the table and spare chair so I could sit down. I finally sat down. Sorry. One stop later two elderly women join our train table and I ask them if it's OK if they don't squish the painting up on the high rail as when it falls it will smash and that won't do as it's a gift for Mum. I say sorry. And I think like this for a while inside my brain whilst sliding the painting between my feet under the table and audibly mumbling sorry several times when it touches the lady's shoe. Sorry. I don't want to smash the glass on this painting. Sorry. I don't even know why I am saying sorry anymore just sorry, OK everybody, fucking sorry. I am fucking sick of saying sorry. My new jumper is too hot. Thick wool. I am hungry and thirsty. I am sweating. I have a headache. I am having a weird period. I didn't eat yet today. I am knackered. Fucking hell. Sorry. Sorry for myself.

Sorry. I stand up by the doors. The train is approaching my stop. Sorry I say to the two schoolboys because I have been thinking about how much I say sorry and I find I'm unintentionally standing in front of the button you have to push to make the door open. I say sorry to the schoolboys and they push the button and the doors open and we are on the platform. As I get off the train I see an old friend I have not seen for over twenty years boarding the train. I wave. Hello I say. I don't say sorry. But as I walk towards the station exit I am sorry I have lost touch with her. Sorry.

I wait for a cab and it takes ages and it's cold and it's getting dark. I get in the cab and say sorry to the cab driver for giving my mum's address wrong the first time. Once I am at my mother's I say sorry I am so late. Sorry. She makes tea. We sit and wait for the kettle to boil. I am starving. She tells me that I have put weight on. Sorry I say. I am so hungry. And also I am sorry I am getting fat. I'm having a weird period. And I'm bloated. And hot. I am perimenopausal which is basically being menopausal with random and irregular periods and being sorry all the time. And she says no you aren't. I say sorry, yes I am. She says you're not allowed to be perimenopausal it makes me feel old. Sorry Mum, I say. Sorry she says. Sorry if it makes you feel old that I'm getting older Mum. Guess what? Menopause makes me feel old, too. Sorry it makes you feel old, too, Mum. We laugh and drink tea and dunk biscuits which will make us fat. Not sorry. Then we have a fag and we make apologies about the fact we stopped and started smoking again.

Not smoking as much as we used to. No. But we still do smoke sometimes. And she is sorry. And I am sorry, sorry, but we still share a fag. It's bad for us. And we agree it is bad and we shake our heads and feel sorry for our lungs. Sorry. We start laughing again. I tell her I just cannot say sorry anymore today. And I laugh. And she laughs. We laugh loads. We change the subject and it's my mum and my sister and me, just drinking tea and eating biscuits and chatting and laughing at my kid sister, who is never sorry but often very funny.

Do Not Mistake This Smile

as yours to keep. Do not see this heart as
expendable. Do not mistake hesitation for
fear. Do not confuse softness for weakness,
empathy for weakness, generosity for weak-
ness. Do not mistake kindness for weakness.
Do not mistake joyfulness for foolishness or
excitement for immaturity. Do not mistake
passion for blind faith. Do not mistake this
love for this life for idealism. Do not imagine
you can crush or squash this. Do not try to
undermine this. Never underestimate this.
Do not piss on my fire. Do not rain on my
parade. Do not use my name like a ticket.
Do not tell me this is all there is and all you
have to give, when we know there is more,
you are capable of more, you are just hoping
someone else will go first and do the heavy
lifting for you. Do not confuse big love for
a free-for-all. Do not expect others to do all
the dreaming for you, you must dream your
own dreams. Hope is a group project: please
share the work of hope or there is no hope.

October Tape Experiment

One October, a very long time ago, I taped
the whole month, I worked and lived and
loved, I ate and drank and slept, but all whilst
recording everything I was doing:

typing poems on a typewriter,
performing in boozy bars,
drinking in the Colony in Soho,
playing guitar in the dark alone,
flirting on the telephone,
eating dinner with a friend,
taking a train to visit Mum.

Me and my Dictaphone – we did a lot of
walking, smoking, thinking, drinking, writing
and yet more walking – Hampstead Heath
to Kentish Town to Camden to Regents Park
to Soho to Southbank to Waterloo, the red
light flashing in my top pocket, recording an
audio loop, capturing an era. The sounds of
my life, my breath, the busy traffic, the people
I knew back then, the era and changing times.
I still have the cassettes of that October in
a box, which I sealed shut.

Now, something about the October light and the way I feel this morning reminds me of that time, and that one October making those particular, peculiar recordings and writing experiments. It was long before social media and smartphones. I guess it was a little like a selfie, but audio and not for sharing. I suppose I was exploring and memorising our world through sound, making a time machine of sorts, a way to hear who and where we were. I made a month of tape recordings:

the clip-clop of my cowboy boot heels,
the crunch of autumn leaves,
running for a bus, the sounds of the bus,
drinking in a bustling and smoky pub,
someone asking, 'Why are you recording this?'

I remember that strange month, sad month, odd month. I remember listening to these tapes and hearing my boot heels clicking on the pavement, then being surprised by voices, how many kind people called out and spoke to me as I walked around my London: *Hello Salena*, they said, *Alright, mate!* Sometimes they called my name like this, *Hello Salena*, passing someone crossing a busy street, *Hello*, as you bump into someone in a pub. *Hello Godden* they'd say on these tapes —

not knowing I was observing my life in audio, not knowing my pockets were stuffed full, spare batteries, blank tapes, a notebook and pen.

I was a little scientific and analytic about it. But I was also quite smashed a lot of the time, so I would make mistakes, flip a cassette tape over and record over the same side twice or forget to change the batteries and lose some crucial evidence, events and late hours. It was pot luck what actually got recorded and saved and what was lost forever. I know I was behaving unnaturally, performing, sometimes thinking I was being clever, knowing I was on tape, telling people they were on tape and us all performing to the tape. Telling folk it was a wild experiment. And people would change the way they spoke to me. Or react as though I was a journalist interviewing them. All the time I wondered: How much of life is a performance? What is real? Authentic? True? Why do we change when we know there is a recording of our idea of self?

Each morning I would wake up and make tea or pour a beer and smoke fags and record myself listening to the recordings from the day before and type poems and write diaries about the audio content: how it made me feel, what or who was I hearing. Writing and processing the images and emotions and soundscapes I'd captured. These morning poetry sessions and recordings became a loop of the days before-before-before and the typing-typing-typing and the sound of writing-writing-writing. A mirror looping into a mirror looping into a mirror. I remember I wrote about the sound of October and the autumn leaves and my adventures in Soho and all the people I'd bumped into and chatted and drank with the day before. I wrote about performance, how we perform when we don't need to. What is real and what is unreal. What is expected? If nobody is looking, are we more ourselves to ourselves? In pubs and bars (for I was mad and young and out drinking every night) I would tell people, *I am recording my life on earth, it's a poetry experiment* and notice them begin to either shout and perform for me and the tape, or go quiet and change when they knew, I knew, they knew they were being recorded.

I forgot about it until now. I'm not going to open the box, not this year. Maybe in another ten years' time. I know the box is down in the basement, but no, not now, I won't open it now, it is enough to know it is there, sealed and dusty, it is good to know it is down there. I am gazing out of my window at the orange leafy October light and remembering it and that era.

I recall one tape: I'm with my mum in an M&S changing room as she is making me get fitted for a new bra. We are laughing. It is a moment of intimacy and love. And on another tape I'm with Oli, we're drinking absinthe up high on the edge of the Hastings cliffs and singing death wishes into the abyss. I want to jump into the stormy sea. I record a taste of loss. Now we are here, and in this October, and the leaves

still

fall.

If We Listen to the Ferocious Child
and All That Ferocious Love
and Love the Child Ferociously

Why are you leaving the child sitting on the
doorstep in the cold? That poor hungry child,
why do you leave her there waiting, forever,
waiting? What is she waiting for? Why don't
you open the door, invite her into your home,
can you do that for her, can you bring her in,
can you invite her into your kitchen? And what
would you say to her, what can you see, can
you see how hungry and cold she is? Come on,
take her into your home, make her warm, wrap
her in a blanket, give her some sweet tea, give
her bread and jam, show her your room, show
her your books, does she love books? Of course,
she's delighted, she loves stories, just as much
as you do, and what would you say to her, what
does she say to you, what does she want? Can
you try and imagine it, can you listen to her,
can you hold her, will you hug her, and love
her, love her, she is you, of course she is, she
was always you, she is hungry, she is waiting on
a cold doorstep for you, so open the door and
let her in and love her, love her, love her.

Grandmother

When grandmother died she took her secrets to her grave.

Now, looking back, I can see how all her life she protected unsaid things. She stood by tradition; a lot of people of that generation still do. She made sacrifices, she put herself last. She put sons before daughters, she put her faith in men and the very patriarchy that enslaved her. She was loved, she was dignified and fiercely proud to the end, and keeping up appearances meant everything to her.

When grandmother died she took her secrets to the grave.

We knew she was getting old and sick and that her time was coming, but it was still a shock when she was gone. She had power and influence over us all. She died believing in everything she had been told since childhood, those old family values and ideals, church and tradition, she believed in it all, and that meant we all had our parts to play in this strange pretence, an uncomfortable charade. We all said it was the end of an era when she died, we knew it was also the end of the quiet, the end of her protection.

The truth will surface now and that's for sure.

Burned

It is a bloody drama
someone will shout out: *Witch!*
then the first lit match is thrown

it is such shame
that it's a young and pretty
finger that will point first

a soft hand she once held true
betrays her, pours on gasoline
and blows and fans the flame

she will mark her cheeks bloody
and surge towards the stars
to claim the whole sky as hers

whilst stamping on charred bones
and twitching black bodies
she will climb to get a better view

of her own pretty reflection
and she'll like herself up there
she'll feel entitled to it

never remembering
that she too might be
burned, any day, soon

it is a bloody drama
someone will shout out: *Witch!*
then the poison spreads

her door is kicked in
she is dragged from bed and thrown
then shaved bald and left to shiver

with humiliation, betrayal and rats
and then on the day of the trial
which is a mockery and more

for theatrics than justice
see another pretty finger pointing in
judgement and know all is lost

see twisted crossed arms
hard pale faces in neat rows
demanding that she be condemned

there are no kind faces there
neither in defence nor accusation
which is a pity but no shock

how folk keep quiet to protect their own
how they find her guilty quick and clap
and jeer as she is tied on top of the pyre

dry wood splintering beneath bare feet
sneering grins, crowds cheer, drink beer
first wisp of smoke curling

and then a
scream of
violent heat

but above her,
the sky, vast,
cold mint-blue

she'll see it
and take that last gasp
of cool spring air

before plumes
of black smoke
and shadow and death

orange flames bite
her feet and legs and
fire starts devouring its meal

and she's so disappointed
in herself in this moment
even as she burns to death

it is herself
she is most
annoyed with

above everything
it is her own self
she is most angry with

she should have fought harder
she should have protected herself
she should have made her light dull

she spoke a truth and now she is
burning to death, it's violent and it hurts
she should have kept her mouth shut

she should have made her heart silent
she should have kept her ideas to herself
it was madness to live so bold and bright

but she knows
that would have been
a life lived untrue

her screaming flesh
how she burns and burns
and it is too late for prayer

then she is ash, free in the wind
as a name is always a name carried on
the years that follow speak the truth

the centuries will do work left undone
a lock of hope might be found
perhaps a diary or some letter

but someone will discover
the paper trail she left and a
granddaughter of a great niece

will find a poem and put up a statue
(it will be grey-stone ugly but
it's the thought that counts)

and people will fight about it
then it will be forgotten and
covered in ivy and pigeon shit

her ash in the wind
whispering in the trees
spirit as memory as dream

it is all too sad, you know
what happens next
you know how it goes

you mark my words
history teaches us
someone must pay

a woman is burned.

Egg and Spoon Race

Imagined babies, lost babies, ghost babies, accidental babies, false alarms, trick questions, how we are all mother, auntie, sibling, teacher, carer, we nurture, we feed, we do the work, the emotional labour. There we share miscarriages, complications, abortions, near misses, borrowed babies, weekend babies, the babies that are yours for as long as you are the girlfriend or lover or wife or partner. We are mother a dozen times in a hundred ways. We do the finger painting, warm the milk and watch cartoons. We chase naked bodies with pyjamas, there are nappies and tears and patted backs, and all the tantrums and crying and teething, the smell of baby powder, yes, I know it, and I know all the nursery rhymes. I have dreamed things I dare not say and felt things I had no words for. I have longed and hurt and cried and bled. Of course I have. Once I tore this question apart and made a choice that was mine to make. I said a no and no is a sentence. I broke the egg and the yolk rushed into the sea and I sank in that salt water deliberately. I prayed over a toilet bowl, holding a split condom, forced to see the truth in the shadow and once I pushed with fear and pain, then lay silent and alone in all the black and the rain. I listened as my ancestors howled in the wind, and I wept, like so many, I wept, and then we kept it all nice and shush, we don't talk about all that, that's a shushed thing. Sometimes we just don't know what to say, so we take the snide comments, we nod politely, you are quite right, we did the egg and spoon race wrong. I am bad at the egg and spoon race. And I don't do a school run every day, I don't sew name tags into gym kits, I don't have to go to a parents' evening, I don't have to find money for trips to the zoo, I don't cut apple slices for new teeth, don't, won't, can't, shan't, but this phrase you like to use, childless. Less? Child-free, OK perhaps free, but never less, not less, not ever less, no. I think it is quite rude to look at a person and assume they don't know their path, that they haven't thought about it, considered their options and choices. Everyone I know has their fair share of love, grief and fury, nightmares and fairy tales, mistakes and accidents, loss and heartbreak, lots of *what if*s and *but*s. The world would be a kinder place if everyone remembered this, that we are all different, we can, we couldn't, we would, we wouldn't. Listen, some people just don't do the egg and spoon race. And that is perfectly fine and OK and thank you.

So, Can You Tell Me About
Your Creative Process?

After a long hot bath
they sit on the edge of the bed
wrapped in a damp towel
they stare into space and then
burst into tears and hate everything
because it all hurts and feels wrong
they get cold and shiver
in the shadow of self-doubt
drowning in waves of self-loathing
they will tell themselves
that they have nothing left to give
that life is pointless
and that books are stupid
and who gives a shit about poetry?
they do, they cry, *they do*
they give a shit about poems
and then they will cry even more
because it is a bit sad how much
they care about poetry
and then they cry about that
until there are no more tears left
and there is nothing else to do
but dry the tears and
write it, write it, write it.

4 a.m. Writing Club

It is 4 a.m.
I write a letter
I'll never post
in soft blue light
of dawn and old rain
I type:
Goodbye
Dear autumn
Dear fox
Dear roses
end of a chapter
the last page rustles
with brown leaves
the spiders arrive
on a Monday
they tell you to
pick your fights
they say:
Don't break the thread
open the windows
and let the fly fly
acceptance.

Seasons change
and you, my darling,
change with them.
The clouds white
as handkerchiefs
waved in surrender,
come on then, winter,
do your icy worst,
you and me
we never were
any good at this,
so, we hibernate
and write and
write and write
until the light
returns.

This Virus

On the radio
a doctor says
'this virus
will not
get bored'
and now I
keep imagining
this virus
like a
petulant teenager
a grumpy little brat
a pain in the ass kid
having tantrums
and yelling
'boring'
every time
someone says
wear a mask
'boring'
wash your hands
'boring'
take care
'boring'
stay safe
'boring'
love you.

All You Have to Do Is Care

about it so much you work on it every day and some days
you work a little and other days you work a lot and some
days it will come easy and other days it's too much but all
you have to do is care about it and care so much you want
to touch it and taste it and work on it every day all day
and there are times you watch the sun rise and you will
wonder why you get up so early and care about it so much
and there are tears and laughter and you get a bit mad in
there and lonely and weeks pass months pass sometimes
years pass but finally you think you have something you
really care about so you somehow find some courage and
show someone and you tell them you care about it and you
tell them that you care about it an awful lot and you feel
afraid but you ask them to look at it and if you're lucky
they care about it too and they might even tell someone
else about it and soon maybe two or three different people
might start caring about it and that is a great feeling isn't
it and literally a dream come true that three or maybe four
people in the world like a thing you made and care about
and then these people might tell other people and then
maybe they'll care about it too and some of them might
write about it and say they care about it and then people
will read that and hopefully begin to care about it too and
that's so generous and also so intense now because the next

thing you know maybe lots of people begin to care about the thing you care about lots of people you never even met care about it people you don't even know care about it and people might start talking about it and caring about it and that is wonderful and you feel excited and strange and vulnerable all at once as something glorious is happening and the thing you cared about and shared is making other people feel moved or happy or inspired or connected somehow and well that's amazing and then suddenly there are people with their thoughts and feelings and opinions about the thing you made and everyone has their own perspective on the thing you care about and not everyone gets it or likes it or even cares about it and that is incredible to you and terrifying because you cannot control whether people care about what you care about and they let you know whether they care or not whilst you still remember when it was a secret and all yours and you were the only one who cared about it and you remember how you once believed you were the only one that would ever care about it and you remember it as a flickering flame of an idea that lived in your head and heart and you remember the tears and the laughs and the lonely madness it took to write it down and make it and that's so beautiful and crazy how it feels so long ago because now it is a thing that is shared and some people let you know they care and others let you know that they do not care about the thing you care about and others are very busy caring about their own thing right now because not everyone cares about all the same things at the same time and you know not everyone cares about the things you care about and this is a gamble and a connection and a sharing of alchemy and magic and making things you care about depends on luck and fate and courage and it begins to feel like you are on a non-stop speeding train and you can see the sky above and the fall below and the destination is constantly changing and you never know who is on board or in another carriage and you don't know who is driving this train or if it is OK to smoke so you roll the window down and stick your neck out and have a cigarette anyway and you enjoy the ride for a while and the view is a blur of urgency and you feel a mixture of hopeful and glad and grateful and anxious and you are on this great electric sky-train adventure on a thin glass track with bright flashing lights and loud fizzy talk and the thing you care about changes shapes in other people's coffee-breathed mouths and it twists in the words like a kite and then suddenly one morning you just jump off the train and you watch it fade smaller and smaller into the distance and you let it go and you walk all the way home barefoot and humble and you quietly shut your door and you feel a jumble of tired and happy and sad for a while and you feel emptied and you may get drunk and stare up at the stars and ask the moon why you care so much and why you took it all so seriously and you know it is because you care deep down and so you laugh at yourself and you cry a little too and eventually you eat something sensible and you grumble a bit and put yourself to bed early and you dream and dream and dream and you dream about caring about things and then you wake up in the middle of the darkness and watch

day break with a spectacular sunrise and you have a sensa-
tional feeling and in that moment it is all yours and in that
minute you truly live as you care about some tiny detail in
some colour or sound or feeling and you pick up a pen and
write one word and then another word and then another
and you start working in silence and solitude in that first
light that is golden and warm and it is beautiful because
that is the best time of all times because you care about it
and it is all yours and new and shiny and all you have to
do is care about it and care so much you want to touch it
and taste it and work on it every day all day and some days
you work a little and other days you work a lot but all you
have to do is care all you have to do is care all you have to
do is . . .

A Child Washes Up on the Beach

their corpse
splashed across the news

the sunken wrecks
on waves the mourning song

so many have drowned before
and more will drown tomorrow

salt water holds the truth
a grave of silt and sand

the ocean is a cemetery
with fish for flowers

a child washes up on the beach
a child washes up
a child washes
a child was
a child
a chi
a c
a

With Love, Grief and Fury 3

Winter 2021

Oh, do tell me
what to wear this season:

old pyjamas to peel potatoes
we can barely afford to boil,

threadbare coat to worry and pace
crowded hospital waiting rooms –

and the old boots that stood
alone at the graves of loved ones

will also be worn to march and protest,
singing songs, with love, grief and fury.

Blackbird

I start writing at 4 a.m.
when bony branches tap
against fading starlight.
I'm listening to one
January bird singing
a hungry, cold song.
And it's then I think
I love you,
you,
there in the bed
as you turn softly
to feel me go.
Shush, I say,
Go back to sleep.

I leave your warmth
to shiver at my desk
and write this poem
about now and January
and the blackbird
and the tapping of
branches against first light.
I'm capturing this hour
in my tea cup.

I write
I love him
because
when I ask for his advice
he never suggests
the easy or cheap route
the fast or smooth path
always it's the big thing to do

he says,
look for the big thing to do,
and it's often difficult but
he's often right.

It's 7 a.m. when
I put down my pen
and slide back into bed,
I hold him close and
feel him stir and rise,
there he is and there we are,
it's the start of the day
the beginning of a new year
and love is the big thing to do.

We Will Write Poems About You When You Are Dead

And they will be the saddest and most beautiful poems. And all the pages wet with tears. And all the loss and longing. And all the agonies drenched within. Oh, yes! We will write such sad poetry about you when you are dead. We will write of you when you are gone and there is no more you. We will write poems soaked in how much we felt for you. We will be sobbing, the paper, all wet with all of our tears. How we will remember your laughter and how you were so you. And all that love and time that was lost. Oh! How it will all echo and empty itself, salt tears into dark ink. And it will wash blue all over the world. A wave of all that we lost, all that want and all that is gone and past. And it will howl up to the full moon, who will turn her pretty face and be eclipsed with these darkest mourning-hour poems. So sad. So very sad will the poems be, that we will write about you when you are dead. The poetry will be a heart obliterated. An explosion of loss. Poetry made of lost and broken things, feathers and pebbles, dried petals and dripping candle wax. This poem will be the universe stopped. But, you are alive now, so we will forget to write you back. We get too busy to talk on the telephone. We cancel arrangements. The weeks pass and then the months. And then we feel weird that so much time has passed since our last letter. Until it is just too awkward. Too strange to make contact and to speak with you. Until many years will pass since we had any contact. We missed your call. You missed our call. Then many more years will pass. We didn't respond to that message. And yet more time passes. But we will think of you often. Always on your birthday, funny, how we never forget your birthday, and then we wonder how you are, where you are. But it will always be too awkward to pick up the phone or to write to you. One day we might eventually try to make contact again, but it will be too late, the wrong hour, the wrong time zone, the wrong date, and then we discover you deleted that address, changed your number, you emigrated or joined a cult or something. So there is no way to contact you anyway. And so there is no point trying. And there is nothing more we can do. Until time does a cruel thing, and we have confirmation that you are dead. And you are gone. And then we will gather together and wear black and stand in a musty chapel and drink in a pub. There will be egg sandwiches, sausage rolls on paper plates, crisps in a bowl. We'll raise a glass, our tears shining in our old eyes as we gaze on photographs and tell each other all we never said and all we never told you and just how much we love you.

Our Anarchy

I'm daydreaming, how I might slow down and mellow with age and write easy poetry about the happy little dog on my knee and the pale lavender sky and the soft snow. How maybe, one day, I will stop writing so much protest poetry, stories soaked in trauma and rooted in our grief, our anarchy, our hopes for humanity, but then I remember I live and write in the 2020s and the world is frightening and I am me and here we are. Still, I often wonder what poems we'd write in a more peaceful time, in another reality, another era; work made from a place of freedom and creativity and not in response or defence, nor in anger or fear. Oh my loves, what dreams we dare to dream, what beautiful books we write. Imagine what art could look like, our theatre and music, what lyrics we'd sing that were about anything but this brutal and divided world. Oh, to create in a safe and gentle space, a kind and listening world. Oh, to write poems about how I love the happy little black dog, so warm, sleeping on my lap, our breath rising and falling together, the sky outside my window, lilac and dove-blue, soft snow falling, and feel that love and peace within me, how wonderful it would be to live just like this, and write without a shadow.

Bees

One woman speaks a truth we all recognise. She is just one bee. And our emotional chores are socks on floors sorry not sorry work is undone dinner is wine sorry honey my sweet mouth is all bees today one bee flew around the world the bee went viral and bad men flapped hysterical but it settled for nothing it had waited until now hoping we might feel it buzz and now we vibrate with bees all over the world we are buzzing people are buzzing we are buzzing with hands on hips and hands on thighs looking into these dark lies these darkening skies with locked open jaw oh how the bees pour more and more the bees pour out of our wide open mouths the bees pour red raw each bee screaming enough is enough and time's up and sing it sister you know the words it's the same tune different century together we throw back our heads triggered and nudged those hidden truths we store and we roar and roar and the bees pour and pour all the bees and all the bees all the bees and all the bees and all the bees of all they ignore we roar with bees

phones buzz

we stare at screens and share it and we say me too and me too and I believe her and then one by one we stand side by side and we gather and we march and we say we are here we say I believe her and then here come the wildcats and packs of snarling dogs the wolves and prides of lions and gorillas and killer whales and livid octopus in knots and no sir sorry you misunderstood that sound you hear is not a thunder of applause for you no that is a stampede of matriarch elephants coming charging and thumping and kicking and thrashing for every slag slut tart whore sow for every queen bitch hen doe cow and wait she is speaking now . . .

can you listen for once without interrupting?

this fury smashes glass ceilings this feeling this rage it is so familiar and it's an old scab we pick this outpouring this gush of bloody melting lava from the guts of mother oh we remember now oh now come on now try to remember you know how this goes if one of us is silent remember how we are all made silent

if one of us is silent how we are all made silent

so yes love the bees we love the bees but now let us remember the fire born from the flame that man kept hot to burn the witch and the healer and the teacher and the magic is the same fire that now scorches schools and temples in man-made wars made for man's own gain for a man-made church and man-made gods in a man-made world of man-made gold remember the last wish of all of our great grandmothers I'm listening tell me again tell me why my blood boils and what it is that rumbles and knots in my DNA and tell me about bees tell me of the unwritten and unarchived and tell me of my warrior and my goddess tell me of my queens and their bloodied dreams of freedom

how it starts with just one bee with one voice brave enough to speak up and remind the hive of stolen honey and all those hours of labour tell me all about the bees all the bees and all the bees and all the bees and all the silenced and all the madnesses and all the cures for hysteria and witchcraft and all the times they call you crazy for feeling this when staring back down the tunnel of time at all the erasure and the yawn of centuries of being exhausted of being distracted of being tired of being told to sit still and be nice and quiet and good and sit pretty on Papa's knee and wait for your turn to speak and wait for a sweet treat but the bees say now is a good time and the bees say time is now yes now is a good time now is a good time now is a good time we are the change and the change is now and we are the now we are the bees we are one we save the bees we save ourselves we save the bees we save ourselves

so buzz bitches buzz

You Used to Know All
the Numbers Off by Heart

You forget things.
Age and time fades the edges,
it's all water under the bridge,
a blur of faces, names and numbers.
The details get fuzzy as the years go by,
you accept you will forget things.
But nobody told you about this,
forgetful fizz and head traffic,
they call it brain fog or something . . . I forget.

But through the mists some astonishing details,
a rush of remembrance and recollection.
Faces and voices and flashbacks,
some unhelpful and uncalled for,
things you thought you'd forgotten,
until your subconscious randomly yells:
Hey remember . . . 438456

and you're just trying to remember
where you put your glasses
or what you went upstairs for.
And you stop and sit on the bed,

your head flooding with time,
and you sit on your bed
and do a whole load of
forgiving and forgetting –
and your glasses are
on your head.

You Made a Fuss

The last time you were here you made a fuss. You didn't like it. You didn't do it right. You didn't relax. Maybe you had an anxiety attack. Or something. The last time you were here there were three of them. Three? Two female nurses and one male nurse. They told you to go behind the curtain and get naked from the waist down and lie on the bed. And then they came around the curtain and all three of them looked at you naked underneath. And you wished you had shaved or tidied up a bit. You were a bit bushy and self-conscious about yourself with your legs open. Then they told you that two of them were in training and the other was here to show them what to do. Or something. So you had to lie there feeling weird. Six eyes peering down, looking down into your furry fanny. You said nothing. They said nothing because they are trained to say nothing. They talked amongst themselves. You didn't like it. You were there for a check-up. You were hoping to have a conversation. You wanted to talk to a doctor about irregular periods. You were starting perimenopause early, but you didn't know that then, because nobody would talk with you about it. But next thing you know you were naked on a paper sheet. You felt the metal and the rubber gloves. Three nurses down the business end and having a good look. You felt bad for feeling bad. You felt bad for getting up inside your head. You felt bad for feeling alarmed, unsettled, you wanted to act like it is perfectly natural to have a tube stuck into you and let medical professionals have a poke about. But you felt tense and nervous. Muscles cramped. Not relaxed. You made a fuss. You had a panic attack. Or a flashback. Both. You couldn't breathe. Or think. You started squirming and freaking out. It was horrible, horrible, horrible. The squeak of the speculum stretching open made you nauseous. You clenched your jaw, feeling strange and seasick and dizzy, weird head rush and then tears, tears filled your eyes. The horror of it. Oh god and the embarrassment. The worst thing is to not be cool and relaxed. The worst thing you can do is to cry and make a fuss. And you made such a fuss. The nurses told you to breathe as they continued looking and judging and poking and thinking thoughts. They probably hated you, you thought they must hate you. You are supposed to relax. You are supposed to not care, you are supposed to trust the nurses. But you were on high alert, you were in a state of alarm. You were too vividly there in the room and present with a tube up your cunt. Heart pounding in your chest. You said ouch and then you said ouch again and louder this time. Because it hurt and they were all having a go and a good poke about. Then you apologised for it hurting. You said sorry. You kept trying to look at the ceiling and pretend you were a car and they were tinkering about in the engine. Sorry you said again. Sorry. You said sorry that they hurt you. Sorry. Sorry, you said, sorry I'm such a crybaby. And they scolded you a bit and told you to breathe and to just relax. One nurse said breathe, again. As another nurse pricked your inner thigh with something. You said ouch. You said sorry again. Sorry. And then sorry for saying sorry. Then you know what you said: Stop. Actually. Can you stop. STOP. Actually. Can you just stop. STOP. Get off me. I don't care if you are in training. And there was a really weird-weird-weird vibe. You said, I want you to stop please. You made a fuss. You were a bad patient. They stood back as you jumped off the bed and got dressed. Tears on your cheeks. Shaking. You wept all the way home. Yes. The last time you were here you made a fuss. Hello. You hand in the form. Shit. It's the same nurse at the desk. Shit. She recognises you. Yes. You know she knows you. Shit. She smiles, she smiles, she smiles. She remembers you. And you remember her. She knows you have a bushy one. She knows you are a screamer, a wriggler, a thinker. She knows you might freak out and think thoughts. She knows you won't know how to relax. She knows you forget to breathe. She knows all about you. She knows you made a fuss. She knows you are the one who says sorry, then says sorry for saying sorry. She takes your file and disappears down the corridor. You think she has gone to get her two friends. Shit! And you have a bushy one again today. You are waiting in the waiting room and starting to sweat. Heart thumping in your chest. You are scared of these nurses. You type this into your phone: The last time I was here I made a fuss.

The Then and the Now

Everyone left a piece of music that will always remind me of our time together. It is sad when people go. It is a pity when friendships end or fade or die. But people don't owe you a lifetime — people don't owe you forever. It happens: you grow apart. You grow distant. People move city or change job or fall in love or change direction. You must accept it, how people take their friendly face with them, take their lovely smiling face to meet another smiling face. People go — leave you and take their curious souls to sunnier shores. Or to cold graves. Going and then gone. I think accepting this takes a lot of work. I hate endings. I loathe goodbyes. But when people are gone, and I mean really gone, and when I know I won't see someone again, or that I cannot see them again, or they are dead, or I am dead to them, and it's truly goodbye, and final, and over and done and gone — well, it's the music that brings them back to mind every time. I'll hear a song, their song, that song, and remember them then and stop in my task — it is never when you expect it.

Picture this: I'm scrubbing a cheese-encrusted oven dish that I baked a delicious pasta in the night before and a song comes on the radio, and in that moment I wonder do they hear it too? Can they feel it too?

Do the dead and the faraway hear music? And as I scrub at this dish, I find I am thinking: Is this music on a radio somewhere near where they are too? Can they hear this tune where they are? If they can, do they also hear this one song, then will they also stop still as this melody plays . . . And with that perhaps we stop at the same time and put down our now. Turn the tap off. Soapy bubbles on the hands. Steam on the window. I just stop still and gaze ahead into the ordinary morning light, utterly transfixed in a memory.

Hey, I remember that song! Hello. I think, hey, they are playing that song. Our song. Hear that!? How that one song transports me right back to you and a time before. I haven't seen your face in my mind for such a long time. I wonder where you are. I hope you are OK and well and wise and free and happy. I hope it is good and peaceful where you are. And I smile a bit and I sigh a little. Maybe you will hear the song and smile a bit and sigh a little too. Maybe. I fly back, I am hurtling through time. I'm surfing on a wave of memory, flung about in the riptide. For that moment in the chorus I cannot move. I'm there again. I feel it all. Everything. I can smell it. Taste it. Feel it pulsating in the senses, the vibration and the colours of that one moment. I am plunged into a connection. It is as if the song is the sun that has kissed my face. I am freckled. There are goosebumps on my arms. It is as if the tune reached into my chest and changed the beat, the rhythm, the pattern, the drum of my heart. It takes my breath away. Stop.

A song has asked me to stop and remember you right now. Maybe a bit of a conversation I had thought I had forgotten. A fight we had. Of course, I am sorry. A dance we shared. I am glad. A barefoot sunrise, a soul-searching full moon. Some crazy mix of emotions, maybe some guilt or shame or sorrow. Maybe some joy and laughter. Good grief. I know now that I'm lucky to have ever known you. You were one of a kind. One in a million. You were fierce and provocative. You were astonishing. Your song gives me a glimpse into us and a time before. And I notice what is happening in my body. I take a good look at this memory that my brain appears to have archived. Look! See how beautiful we were, so, so bold, so bright, so obnoxious, so good looking, so reckless. We were idiots. What strange choices we made. What odd habits we had and bizarre language we shared. We threw the time away. We drank so much. We could have died. No, seriously, we nearly killed each other. My brain floods with a feeling, the shape of dreams made real. Your song is like a photograph pushed beneath my nose, here, a vivid image of us. That tune!

Ah! I listen and I sing along and the words get caught in my throat. I still know the words though. I hear us singing it. I see us dancing, and our young supple bodies and our uncontrollable laughter. And I laugh too. I see the mess we were. I see us. I see how we were desperate and hungry and poor and raw and vulnerable and beautiful. We were survivors of the worst-case scenarios. Your song sweeps me away, this music pulls me under the surface. I am running down the up escalator. Your song is a meteor, smashing the past into the present, a speeding train in flame. Your song holds my hand in the dark, gives it a squeeze and then lets it go. Your song says you are gone. Your song will always be your song. That song, crackling embers, that feeling, as the song ends, the image fades. How that that was then then. And this is now now.

That's when the song finishes. My heart hurts. My eyes hot with tears. I only then realise I'm here. I take a breath. I stopped breathing because I was inside the remembering, I was remembering too hard to breathe. I remember then that I am just remembering.

And that that was then then. And this is now now. I turn the hot tap on again, put my hands in the soapy warm water. The heat brings me to the present. The soap is lemon-scented. The morning light is all daffodils and yellow. Spring is coming tomorrow or soon. I come home to the present, like nothing happened, but love.

Evergreen Tea

Twelve flashes from a menopause diary

1

Hang on. What is this? I am different . . . but the same. What is this thing? This monster? And what is this obstacle, what is this uncertain path, because, well, it seems to me, just as we know ourselves, yes, just as we know our bodies, just as we have found our path and learned our way through, the woods suddenly grow cold and strange, darkest evergreen. For decades we know our cycle, we know our own sex and bodies, and we say, yes, I know these woods, I trust myself here, but now, suddenly, see how the forest is changed and now all deep pools and thick brambles and nettles, and we are told to drink nettle tea and so we drink the tea, evergreen tea, and sip the truth of it and we drink sage tea too, yes tea, love tea, all the tea, and the truth of it, the truth is in the tea, but what really is this . . . change?

2

I keep forgetting people's names. I forget people I have known for years. I stand there blinking and lost even though I know this is you and this is me and please can you be patient for a moment because I'm so hot right now and this night is long and loud, with heat and sweat and this deep red water and this flash flood and this blood and then no blood and then ache and then the ghost blood and the trick of a one-day show and then no show for months and then a flooding and the bed is waves of it and waves of it and what is happening to me? I don't leave the house without a bag stuffed with tampons and pads and clean pants and a mask and gloves and diving equipment and goggles and tissues and waders and armbands, just in case, just in case, just in case of what? Oh the shame of it, I am afraid of the shame, what is this new fear and tears and more tears, as I write this I am crying again and I am roaring my eyes out, Chaka Kahn is on the radio, she is singing *I'm every woman* and the song feels so different today and poignant and yes Chaka, I hear you, I'm every woman, it is true: I'm every woman, I'm every woman, I'm every woman . . .

3

OK. HOT. Slow down for one hot minute hot minute HOT because hot HOT because it's HOT. So I open the fridge and stick my head in it, because it is cool like the longing for an evergreen forest. What is this strange behaviour? Why is it so hot? I am boiling in my own blood. I am a boiled ham. I am in a bubbling pot of feelings. So tell me now what is this? This thing we cannot get any answers for and this thing that is happening to me and in spite of me? Does anyone care? No. Not really. Nope. OK so we must cope and we must manage and we must struggle on our own and we whisper a new secret word we read: PERIMENOPAUSE. It is easy to remember because it is the bit before menopause but with extra peri-peri pepper sauce and so that explains the heat.

4

So finally, tonight, you share your burden at full moon with a bottle of rum in the kitchen with your best friends and you say, Sister, are you going through this too? Yes! She says Yes! Yes, oh thank fuck, I thought it was just me, so what the fuck is this? This rising power, this mighty rage, and what is this intolerable heat? It is called a hot flush. A HOT FLUSH? They call it a hot flush? Well, I'm on fire. I feel like I ate a volcano. I'm bubbling lava and my head is all flames, I'm a walking burning witch. But we must carry on as normal and say excuse me, darlings, can you smell smoke? Please don't mind this wildfire inside me. We don't talk about it. Sister is wise, she tells me to boil herbs, fresh parsley, sage and thyme and use old magic. Drink more water. I cleanse and I clear a path inside myself but inside I feel prickly. There are tigers in my blood. So we simmer a leaf and drink the tea, anxieties thriving in the weeds and undergrowth. I steep herbs, drink the tea, and how does it taste? Honestly? OK it tastes a little bit like drinking a hot salad, hot wet grass juice, but I'll try anything at this point, because I cannot get an appointment and I cannot get any help. I'm a raging maniac insomniac and I'm a volcano and bubbling in my own geyser and I want all the things: I want ice and I want you to touch me and I say *don't touch me* and I don't know what I mean or what I want. I want to jump out of the window into the cold night air, hmm, the wet rainy cold pavement looks inviting. I want to sleep and curl up into a ball like a cool and slimy snail. I want to be held. I want to be alone. I want to hide in a cave and eat cold rocks, delicious chunky crunchy icy rocks and I want to stick smooth rocks down my pants and I want to fill myself with smooth ice and then just walk into Antarctica to feel my feet in the snow and then sink under icy water and die and live like a happy cool-skinned seal, skidding on the ice on my flabby belly into the darkest deepest blue. I want all of this now and all at the same time. Such violent flashing death-thoughts and desperate itchy feelings and too many feelings, feeling all the feelings, die die die, all day long, hot hot hot, feeling all the feelings, all night long, and all the feelings and so what is this? More feeling feelings and more crying. I'll give you something to cry about. Thanks.

5

Perhaps it is a bit like puberty but in reverse. That's what this is, just like puberty, but going in the other direction, you are growing away from being fertile and useful to men, to being useless and invisible. Ah, well now, haha, when you look at it like that, it makes so much sense, that's why they didn't tell us, that's why they don't warn us. Nobody told us, nobody told me. It don't matter. Of course. We don't matter. Hormones go haywire, I feel exactly like a suicidal fifteen-year-old, again, feels so familiar, here are those old dark thoughts, here the childhood death-wishes, here the crying and why am I crying this time? Maybe because the song was sad or because someone was kind or I cried because I was hungry or I cried watching Attenborough and I cried because the world is mad or because my love made me a really nice cheese toastie and I cried because it rained because the rain was the saddest rain and I cried like the rain and I cried because Chaka Khan is so beautiful and I love Chaka Khan and I love that song 'I'm Every Woman'. I'm laughing and roaring with tears all at the same time and looking at the rain being rainy. Furious weather inside me, a tirade of emotion. I am taking everything very personally, all weather is me, wave after wave after wave, smashing me against myself.

6

And breathe. Then here we are. Today there is this calm bit and this very grounded feeling and it is a most gentle breath, and well this is strange and new too, so now what is this? I am wearing new white knickers with no fear of stains, why so much fear of a little blood, I dunno, decades of shame and guilt, but yes, look, see, yes, the bleeding has stopped. Forever. You will never bleed again. Wow OK I think I get it now. So yeah, so no more periods. EVER again. Wow, getting older is amazing and being a big sister, to be an elder, it is an honour. Why was I afraid of this? Is this what's happening now? Some acceptance perhaps? It is a privilege to get older. Say it again. Yeah, OK I think I understand now, I am lucky to get to this age at all. Hallelujah, oh wisdom, oh clever one, oh look at me now, look how I got so wise and jolly and plump and how I am so Zen and wise, I accept it all and oh it must be over and done with now and I think this is what finding balance feels like? I feel like I will be allowed to enter the evergreen forest.

7

I am a machine, my system is rebooting. It brings with it these aching limbs, legs and back and knees and these growing pains and bloated belly and these swollen tits and this forgetful head . . . right now . . . wait . . . am I at Waterloo or London Bridge? Shit! I was writing this in my diary and I totally forgot where I am and all I know is I am in a London train station, and for a good two minutes I blink and stare into space and I don't remember which station this is and I wonder who to ask and if someone can tell me where I am now. Is this brain fog? I feel like I am falling off the world. Falling into fog, thick blue fog. I cannot even see my own hands. Is this London Bridge or Waterloo? I have been here a million times but suddenly I don't recognise the train station. I am lost in my own city. I am lost in my own body. I am lost.

8

Oh great, so I'm just about to go on stage in front of hundreds of people and I am backstage and whooosh blurrrp there's a sporadic random flood, and well yeah, I ruin those new white knickers. Ha! We all know white knickers are a dare, like literally begging the period demon for a random flood of blood from nowhere and with no warning and of course it's a full moon. And now stuff toilet paper down your pants and walk on stage and do a gig like a fucking boss because you are a fucking boss and you have done bloody gigs bleeding bloody blood like this a thousand bloody times, look at you now, oozing in your pants, bleeding on stage, cramps and aches and STILL smashing it and nobody even knows, and nobody even cares. *Hey everyone, you should see what I made red* — not an analogy. Not fair though and such bad timing, hey blood goddess, period demons, we need to talk, we are meant to be on the same team, you are supposed to be my uterus and not my enemy.

9

Hello, Doctor? I know you are busy but I think I want to die a bit. Can you tell me what is happening to me, Doctor? And the doctor says, All women are different, and I say, Hang on, please do not just shrug and tell me all women are different. I think I am bleeding to death, my period won't stop, and, Doctor, I have a job and a life and it's been miles and miles of turmoil and, Doctor, I want to die or sleep, and right now I am not fussy, whichever comes first, the death or the sleep, and the doctor just says, All women are different, and the doctor offers antidepressants, and I say No thank you, and the doctor says, Menopause can last ten years! Ten! Years! So bizarre! OK. Iron deficiency. Eat iron tablets. Eat bags of spinach. Will I live like this for a decade? Every time I ask for help the doctor offers antidepressants. Every time I ask for help the doctor sighs and says, All women are different, the doctor smiles and tells me this again and again, All women are different, the doctor sings, over and over again, All women are different, All women are different, but doctor, I'm every woman.

Doctor, I want to say, I'm every woman, Doctor, do you even know what this feels like? Did you skip this class? I am seeking balance and I am on a journey. I am returning to the land before blood and it hurts. One day I am going to be free in the forest and reconnect with who I am, who I was, who we all were before expectations, before we were useful, Doctor. I am going to be free, I look forward to my freedoms, Doctor. I honour this biology and chemistry that is naturally happening inside my body and brain. I understand I am changing, we are changing, and we won't resist it or fight it, because we are going to a different life, one without draining our life force and all our energy into a bloody pair of pants every month. A life without servitude to shame. We will be free! And if we are lucky, perhaps now people will stop asking us about weddings and babies, finally, what a fucking relief. Maybe people will ask about our brains and dreams, our books and art and how nice that will be, and we can talk about other things like travels and adventures and philosophies and passions. We'll be so wise, we are going to return to wonder, and go forward and go back at the same time, back to our original settings and to who we were before we were made useful to society, before we were forced to grow up too quick, before we had to grow sass and defences and fears and before sex and fags and rum and scars and armour, that is what this is, the menopause is exhausting, but it is also an empowerment. This is the ultimate super-power of reinvention and that is what is feared. This is rebirth. This is what nobody told me, this is what they didn't

tell us, this is what they are not showing us. So this awak-
ening, this is why they burnt witches, powerful older women
who knew herbs and maps and stars and time, this is what
they don't tell you, that you are magic, and it is in your
bones and veins and roots and ancestry and one day if you
are lucky, you too will know to find the forest.

II

Freedom from fear is empowerment. Magic is a freedom from
shame. Fear is a cage. Shame is a prison. So now we return
to a place without shame and fear, to the girl who believed in
her power and wonder. We hold hands with ourselves, the kid
who flew in her dreams. We will know ourselves well, the
whole of a soul, and how we were before the world stuck its
fingers in and said *shame* and dug out expectations and said
shame, before they walked into your jammed open mouth and
said *shame* and tattooed the tongue with *shame* and sit up straight
and *shame* and smear the lipstick *shame* and cross your legs and
shame and wait your turn and *shame* and that dress is too short
and *shame* and keep your mouth shut and *shame* and keep our
little secret *shame* and speak when you are spoken to and *shame*
and I'll give you something to cry about and *shame* you are just
a girl and *shame* and *shame* and what a shame you are just a girl.
Shame. Shame. Shame. Oh, what a sham is shame.

Now see how your wings grow stronger every day. To be whole again, feel whole, and see how you may learn to fly. We are all the water and sky and earth and flame, and fierce and soft at once. Sunlight filtering through jade and leaf. Silver hares darting between the trees. Silver hairs. Hello. I am new here. I grow accustomed to changes, explore this new era, this wise excellence, this dark and verdant forest, come and meet me here, please don't be afraid, it is so cool and lush. This is a good place, this age is emerald, viridescent, I sip on the truth of being, becoming evergreen.

Five Words

she was just walking home
she was just walking home
he drove for several hours
before raping and strangling her
and setting her on fire
she was just walking home
she was just walking home
he was nicknamed the Rapist
by his former work colleagues
she was just walking home
she was just walking home
five words, again, five words
she was just walking home
keep counting the five words
deception, kidnap, rape, strangulation, fire
she was just walking home
she was just walking home
mother says to the press
how she would warn her
Don't get in the car
Don't believe him. Run away.
she was just walking home
she was just walking home
she was handcuffed and unable

to defend herself or run
she was just walking home
she was just walking home
how he used his power
how he used his badge
how he used his handcuffs
and a police-issue belt
tight around her soft throat
she was just walking home
she was just walking home
he took his family out
walking in the same woods
he watches his children play
where her body is dumped
her body in a fridge
old fridge in the pond
her bones, hair and ash
where his kids are playing
she was just walking home
she was just walking home
keep counting the five words
she was compliant and obedient
her poor weeping mother said
I am incandescent with rage
her sister said this: *YOU*
disposed of my sister's body
just like it was rubbish
her bravery on the news
the families now ripped apart

it is breaking my heart
five words, again, five words
she was just walking home
she was just walking home
the police gave him warnings
the police gave him uniform
the police gave him authority
the police gave him power
he's given camouflage and shield
but the truth soon surfaces
the dead girls on WhatsApp
police laughing at crime scenes
the murdered black women's bodies
they're not front-page news
until the WhatsApp is found
pictures of these innocent victims
shared for jokes and larks
they were just walking home
they were just walking home
police disrupt a peaceful vigil
and disrespect the public mourning
police won't police the police
she was just walking home
we are just walking home
count five words with me:
protest, unity, outrage, solidarity, justice
we are just walking home
we are just walking home
tell me who protects us

we are just walking home
tell me who protects us
when doing the right thing
we are just walking home
they are just walking home
but those that are paid
to protect and serve us
may kill us and laugh
may get away with murder
end this violence and injustice
end police violence and injustice
she was just walking home
I write this in tears
with love, grief and fury
we are incandescent with rage.

I Will Walk You Home

I'm losing the light
this winter
everything hurts
I will walk you home

happy for everything
every single word
we shared with you
I will walk you home

razor blade
the bloody sky
slashed apart
I will walk you home

I have bandages
and saltwater to
gently bathe the time
I will walk you home

we nurse the sky
and hold your hand
I will walk you home.

Notes on Exit and Extraction

The root is migrating. Your tooth is getting on your nerves.

As she says this, I feel like my dentist is doing experimental spoken word and reciting a poem to me about migration and movement and courage and nerve. She taps my wisdom tooth and I wince as she continues her poetry, *This one is infected and it is affecting your jaw, your ear and eye, everything is connected.* Yes. I think everything IS connected. It is time to let go. It is time to make time. It is time to make space. I need more space. I must discard old things, like this bad tooth.

Don't probe it with your tongue. Please don't poke it with your dirty fingers and above all please fight the compulsion to fill empty holes. Filling time. Filling holes. Filling space. There's magic in this bad tooth. I think I will cast a spell under the blood moon. I'll bury my old tooth with daffodil bulbs, with rose quartz and clove. I will place it where the winter sun will melt the first snow of the year.

This bone is old as blood, as time,
I wash my tooth in cold moonshine.

I haven't had a drink since . . . Dublin. I've been so sober. No wonder I can hear this screaming person inside me. I cry alone. Where am I? I am in pain. Where are you? Inside here. Inside this intolerable pain. Ever-increasing and escalating pain. She says, *ouch.* I say, *ouch.* And for once I have to agree with myself. This toothache really hurts.

Notes on exit and extraction – when you are in pain it is all your own pain and you do not think of other people's pain. When you are in pain, you will not care for the stories of others' pain. You will think only of your own pain in that moment of your pain. Your pain is everything to you, but only to you. Nobody knows your pain like you know your own pain. Pain is painful because it is full of pain. Your pain is your own pain. Nobody can do your pain for you.

Breathe in and breathe out.

Try to imagine someone worse off, somebody somewhere is in more pain than you. You are lucky it is only your tooth and not your eye.

Imagine if eyes were like teeth. Imagine your baby eyes falling out so your adult eyes can grow. You picture your eye all rotting in your skull. All black and jellied. Pain. You picture an eye that is all pain and sharp glass, splinters, chainsaws, razors, bullets, pain, pain, pain. Breathe in, breathe out. Imagine it is childbirth. Clench jawbone. Clench. Push the pain from the infected gum and up through your ears. Breathe in and breathe out. Big breath, good girl. Push the tooth out. Push. Breathe. Push. This too will pass.

Oh, do fuck off . . . it hurts.

The root vibrates, sending SOS flares shooting up to my eye. My cheeks are a swollen parachute. My jaw is clicking like steel boots. My teeth are soldiers marching in soft sore trench gums. My mouth is a battlefield. The searing pain is a He – and He wears a Nazi uniform. He is goose-stepping in my dirty wisdom tooth. I feel the snap of his sharp boot-heels from jaw to temple. You know, I really should write about this: it really is the most extraordinary toothache. I'm a war correspondent and there is a battle inside my head.

Hello, I am live from inside my own mouth. Take more pain killers! Friendly fire! Bombs ahoy!

My dentist experiments with more avant-garde spoken-word poetry whilst poking about in my painful wisdom tooth. They ask me to sign a form. I notice this line:

If the nerve is damaged you might never speak the same way again, it could damage the nerve and alter your speech and your tongue.

I picture future-me doing poems on Radio 4 with a lisp like this: *Shnello shnmy shname shnis Shnalena Shnodden.* Stop it. It's not funny. Too much pain. Too much pain. I cannot think. Too much pain, pain, pain. Send in the cavalry. Rip these offensives from my war-torn skull. Stop thinking so much. So many thoughts and feelings. Take pills. Eat ice-cream. Soft mashed potato for dinner.

Come now, be a brave thing. Today we over-throw the fascist regime in my mouth. Fuck these bigots! Viva the revolution!

In the hospital, my mouth is jammed open, crammed with blue rubber fingers.

The needles poke and prick and something rubber snaps. *Now relax, breathe, I am just peeling back the gum,* says a voice from behind a green mask. I see the big sharp scalpel. My heart is banging. I hear a rip and squelch. Then a tear and a pop and whoosh.

Hurrah! It is born!

I want everyone in the hospital to cheer! Congratulations! My baby wisdom tooth! Mother and baby are doing well. They stitch me up and give me the tooth to take home. They don't know I intend to use it for voodoo.

When I get home, the first snow falls as white as teeth. Soft milk teeth falling from the sky. I know this tooth trauma will fade into white and then the daffodils will rise, yellow stars and blue skies. And I know my daffodils will bite and chew on winter and gnash down on spiders and snails. *Clackitty-clack* echo my daffodils from beneath the frosted earth. My wisdom tooth cracks open under the bulbs. Tooth once so infected and affected, so sore and raw, now I know my black tooth feeds the flowers and nourishes the earth.

So strange: it is as if the house forgets they share the same gum in the same mouth in the same head. Idiot teeth. These teeth must all learn to live in the same mouth, side by side, just as we all live on the same rock and under the same sky. As I bury my dead wisdom teeth I sing this song:

This bone is old, my blood is mine
I wash my tooth in salt moonshine.
Give thanks, I thrive and live in truth
as true as a moon, so long in the tooth.
This bone is old as blood, as time,
I'll wash the truth in cold moonshine,
in cold moonshine, I wash this time,
may we rise high in spring sunshine.

With Love, Grief and Fury 4

Spring 2020

Last night I dreamt we had two months left and then the world was going to end. There would be nothing, no here, no you, and no me. Many of us swarmed south to the coast to get to Spain – in my dream it was safer than this green bog, this swamped island, we were flooded, surrounded by deadly seawater.

Maybe we should build an ark. The ice caps are melting, the sea levels are rising. Our shipbuilding heritage is in our DNA – the people of Albion are island dwellers, boat people, water and wood, forever connected to our forests, seas, rivers and canals. We don't have enough sun to grow our own tea nor enough land to grow enough wheat to make enough flour to make cake.

These apocalyptic nightmares are regular now. I dream with love, grief and fury. I dream I am in a dark basement of a building and I hold a stranger, we are huddled in terror, just me and this complete stranger. We don't know each other's name, but in these vivid nightmares we hold each other as buildings above us collapse under the weight of tsunami, walls of water, flood, blood, fire. We're all gonna die the way we live. I think I will die holding a stranger.

Whoever you are, I hold you.

But come now, enough solastalgia, let's make tea with the last tea bag from the last delivery, before they shut the borders. Let's bake a cake with the last of the cocoa and flour from the last rations from the last shipment, the last of the gas lit with the last dry match. Let's make merry before all is lost.

All I know is this, my love —
we must change the way
that we only hug strangers
in our nightmares.

Monsters in Spring

It's the first days of spring, pink blossom and yellow sunshine.

Gigging Monster roars and wakes ferocious, looking for a fight with Writing Monster who is quietly working inside a book. Gigging Monster leaps about the house singing, 'Spring is here! Spring is here! Stop writing! You wrote loads all winter, it's my turn, it is my time to dance in the spring sunshine! You better have written something half-decent, because it is me that has to do all the leg work and stand on stage and tour it all summer!'

Writing Monster bursts into tears, upset with all the noise. She runs upstairs and throws herself on the bed and weeps about her need for solitude. She pours on the guilt about unfinished stories, she wails, 'but I like writing, writing is a happy place . . .' Writing Monster is so needy. She demands all of my time and patience. So much re-living and gazing into the long dark night.

Gigging Monster has been locked in a box and sleeping all winter, as Writing Monster wrote books. Gigging Monster is fierce, fixing cocktails, jangling ice cubes and declaring 'Oh, how I need to see poets again, I need fun and I need laughter!' She tells me she has ordered a new suit from the tailors. She wants me to wear this new red lipstick with it. But first she orders me to bathe and wash and comb my hair. Writing Monster likes me in my pyjamas, knotty hair, living on tea and toast.

Gigging Monster likes shiny things, festivals and fires and howling at the moon. Gigging Monster likes travelling and parties and all the buzz of people and late-night chats. Gigging Monster makes her demands, she tells me it is time to get back on tour, she begs for the bright lights of Soho and mischief.

Writing Monster clings to my slippers and weeps, 'Please don't leave me in here . . .' as she shows me a new novel we want to finish.

And here I am stuck in the middle. It is like this every year during the first days of spring. As soon as the light changes, I am thrown about in this battle, a clash of ego and mania, pull and push, dark and light, winter to summer, the conflict of inside and outside, introvert and extravert. There is no rest with my monsters.

Yet it is with wonder that we watch winter end and spring return, my monsters and I, we gather the first miraculous daffodils of the year, every year, we arrange them in a vase placed in the centre of the kitchen table, as though they are the first flowers we have ever seen.

These monsters, these brain bullies, I made them, I feed them, I hold them, I need them, I hate them, I love them, and as the decades pass I am trying to learn to balance them equally.

I Want to Be Your Wife

1

At the end of the day, I want to be your wife. I want to wear a cream satin nightie and sit at my vanity table, rubbing my hands vigorously with hand cream. I will moisturise my hands and my forearms and elbows, and listen as you tell me a thing which is very important then you put down the *New York Times* and take off your glasses to tell me this thing and I will look into the mirror at my reflection and over at you as you lie on top of the bed in your vest and shorts and socks whilst contemplating this important thing. I will pull a paddle brush through my hair, which will be very lovely hair, it will be easy to brush and it will be brushed and brushed and brushed and it is then that I will pause and say into the mirror: *You know what you have to do, you have to kill your boss.*

2

In the morning, I want to be your wife. I will pour fresh orange juice into sparkling glasses from a glass jug placed in the centre of the breakfast table laden with bowls of berries and stacks of pancakes which I prepared, I rinse a cup in the kitchen sink and glance out of the window at the neighbour's ginger cat, I mumble about the damn mangy cat crapping everywhere and then turn and ask about our lake house, *It's been a while*, I say, you nod and tell me you will think about it. You won't have time for breakfast but you pour yourself a coffee from the pot, it is good coffee, expensive coffee, you slurp it quick and as you leave you kiss my cheek, super quick because you need to go, and you're a very busy man. You might take a bite of toast, I hear a crunch, your jaw clicks. The muted television the news: a body has washed up on the beach.

3

I want to be your wife at home doing laundry. When we talk on the phone I will always talk to you whilst holding a full laundry basket on my hip, the phone sits in the crook of my neck, I do not put the laundry basket down, this is part of the wife thing I will do. I would be a good wife and particularly great at these laundry basket phone calls. I will talk of ordinary things: the man came to fix the thing, don't forget we have that dinner next weekend, the neighbour's cat is missing. I tell you I saw the neighbour staple leaflets to lamp posts, and we laugh a little, mangy crappy cat ha ha.

4

I want to be your wife at the end of the day I want to be your wife at the end of the day I am outside the local supermarket I want to be your wife I carry groceries and I want to be your wife I wait to cross the busy road I want to be your wife something is off a grapefruit rolls to the kerb a dog runs into the traffic your boss's body has been identified washed up on the beach I want to be your wife the neighbour's cat has been found hanging in our apple tree I want to be your wife everything is fine I want to be your day at the end of the wife.

Sun Cream in February

You finish writing a book but you don't send it off right away. You sit reading it, imagining being the poet you hope will read it one day. You erase a comma. Then put it back. And then erase it again. You keep wondering — why did you spend this winter writing a book? Because one day we all might burn books for heat. One day we might use books to build rafts. We'll tether books together to sail to safety.

I think maybe the world will end with dead unread books.

You snap your laptop shut. You go downstairs and switch on the TV. The news is on. There are images of empty supermarket shelves. The newsreader is talking about stock-piling food and medicine. They cut to footage of a couple stockpiling tins. The couple stands side by side and they smile into the camera by a wall of baked beans. They grin down the lens and tell us all at home that they are ready. *I'm ready.* The man repeats. *We want to be ready.* His wife nods. *We want to be ready.* They say this in unison as they fill plastic storage boxes with tins of baked beans.

I think the beans situation is covered now thanks to John and Elaine in Maidstone.

At the end of the world, will baked beans be like heroin? You now imagine swapping a book for a tin of baked beans and wonder, which book would you sacrifice for a tin of beans? You picture yourself scoring a cheeky hit of beans on toast by a public toilet. Hey man, got any dirty brown sauce?

You switch off the TV and go into the kitchen to make tea. You stare out of the window at the pink and the sky and the light. It is summer but it is February. But it is summer and it is February. And too bright and too warm and too weird and too sunny. It is alarming that they don't mention this heat on the news. We need sun cream in February. Sun cream in February. And my neighbour is having a barbecue in February. And the last super tusker elephant died this February. And it is summer and it is February and it is summer and it is February.

What was the point of writing a book all winter? What is the point of us? When our time is so fractured. Divided. Distracted. Interrupted. Our attention is demanded and demanding attention. Our world is burning, flooding and changed.

But then if not for love, then why are we all here?

And what is your soul for? If not for books, for poetry, for music, for art, for sharing, for dreaming? Why are we all here? If not for your big glad heart, your joy, for faith and belief and for love love love. If not for your humanity and connection? What else is there? And what are we all getting out of bed for? And what are your eyes for? And what are you looking at? And what do you want? And what is the point of breath if not to sing for freedom and survival and light and colour and joy and you – yes, *you* – what do you march for? And why are you angry? And what are you all fighting about? If not for your planet? If not for the animals? If not for the rainforest and if not for the ocean? If not for the elephants? The last elephants . . .

And if not for all you love, then what was it all for?

Was it really just about baked beans?

Brown Sugar

I'm on a train
watching the world
pass by my window
see the coasts of Devon
West Country fields
a blurring of bluebells
the tea trolley arrives
I order a coffee
the train guard asks,
'Milk? Sugar?'
Then the lady opposite me
she also orders coffee
again the guard asks,
'Milk? Sugar?'
She looks at me
she looks at him
she laughs
then looks me
right in the eyes
and then shouts
'BLACK!
I'm not racist.'
'Ha ha,' she laughs
'I like black coffee.'

Umbilical

You find a photograph of your mother and notice you are older than her now. You might say under your breath to yourself: *I am older than my mother was in this picture.* For the first time then you observe the image as though you have not noticed it before. You are now older than your mother is in this yellowing photograph. You look at her differently. Maybe you notice surface things: her gorgeous hair, her soft face, her clothes and shoes, all of another era. Maybe you know the story of the setting, perhaps you know the room or the garden she is in. Perhaps you know who took the shot and captured this image. But you'll see your mother as a young person of another time and another age. You might notice she is beautiful. Or you might think she looks tiny or lost or scared or innocent. You might think she looks slim or happy or carefree, perhaps, happy because you are not born yet to trouble her sleep and worry her dreams. You might see a little bit of yourself in there, in her face, in her demeanour. You'll look, and I mean really look, at her face in this one photograph and you might see yourself beginning there. A glint of you is in her smile. This might be pleasing. It might disturb you. You might feel protective about it, because without that tiny glimmer you might not have been born, perhaps, perhaps not. But you will know that once upon a time your mother was younger and more innocent than you are now. I mean look at you, with your smartphone and your fast food and your computer, you are modern, you know all kinds of things now, you know a lot of things she does not know and may not understand. You are older now and you know things that you did not know when you were younger than her. It is quite mesmerising, when you think about it. It is miraculous what changes the years bring, what you learn and unlearn, really. But one day you might be lucky, to find this gift of a moment, to find this photograph, to imagine greeting your mother as a younger person, you as the adult and wise person from the future. You might want to forewarn her about your father. You might want to comfort her about her own father. You might wish to thank her and tell her you love her. You might want to cry or laugh a little with her. But if you are lucky, you might be able to very carefully curl your leg up and over and push your foot through the film of time and climb into the photograph. You may be able to slide into the picture, gently, so gently, so you don't upset anything as you step into the frame, just so you can stand by her side. And once you are in the picture, well, then you will see the scene she sees, then you will see everything. You will see what she is smiling at, who she is looking it, who took the photo. And then you might also get a glimpse into the choices she made and the words she spoke and the armour she wore and the world she danced in then. You may see what she sees, I mean, behind and beyond the photographer, beyond the place, the room or garden which no longer exists, beyond where the photograph is taken, beyond the wall and the sky.

You may, for a few brief moments, see her world view, see her parents, see her grandparents, the world she lived in when this one image was captured. You'll hear it and smell the people, your dead family in full colour, the food they eat, the news they discuss, the war and peace, the hardships and challenges they faced. You are in the room and you might hear their laughter and feel it all, her hopes and dreams and triumphs. You may just once, very momentarily, stand still there, quiet, inside the photograph and smell the roses in the garden that isn't there anymore, sit like a ghost in the room in the home that isn't there. Imagine that: you are inside the photograph now. You stand still for the photograph to be taken, you stand beside your beautiful young mother as though you are now her ancestor, a spirit from her future. You might try to hold her hand or put your arm around her young shoulders. As you see what she sees as the picture is taken, as you see beyond the four corners of the photograph. You may look up and see your own adult face, your nowadays face, your older face, staring into the photograph above you. You might see your face in this present looking down at a picture of your mum in the past. You might be able to wave to yourself. You might share in a magnificent feeling that is the blurring of age and time, if you are lucky, you might feel a tug at the thread that never breaks.

Even After the Storm

ever feel like
you are fine there
where you are
even after the storm
the warm sun
the soft blossom
leaf and petals
surround you
time is slow
and spiral
maybe you'll
eat soon
sip water
you stretch
your slow muscle
you feel gentle and
calm and easy and
even after the storm
it is like
nothing happened
but it is then
from nowhere
a heat so fast
a rough hand

grabs you
sudden
you squelch
bubble and spit
cling onto the
nothing
but
air below
your heart
thrashing
you see
mud as sky
as stars
you froth
and bruise
curl up into
your shell
hold your own
as you're catapulted
through memory
and space
a billion lights
you're hurtling
through the air
and flying you
are flying you
are flying and
then falling
and fallen

you land
on some
undergrowth
stinging nettles
and mulch
woody and dark
and fine and well
you are fine there
where you are
even after the storm
the warm sun
the soft blossom
leaf and petal
and maybe that
whatever that was
didn't happen
to your body
now now
you are here
you are alive
you're fine
in one piece
nothing
to cry about
no fuss
no words
just that
was once
something

terrifying
but right now
nothing
you are fine there
where you are
even after the storm
the warm sun
soft blossom
leaf and petal
surround you

Patient Creature

I am a dog
howling in the hallway

I thought with all this silence
I'd be able to write in here

I thought I'd
find the energy

I seek solace in books
I'm trying to read

taking armfuls of novels
from kitchen to sofa

to bath and
back to bed

the real is urgent
the imaginary is a fog

worry is exhausting
I'm too sad to sleep

if I do I only
dream of you

you are in such terrific pain
you tell me they took a tube out

you're sitting up now
you managed some soup

no visitors allowed but
you tell me you dream of me

that I am by your bed
I whisper in your ear

it was not a dream, love
I am with you

I am there and here
wishing you get well

I know you are being brave
and doing what the doctors tell you

you are practical and sensible
you keep telling me you will be OK

you say, they will fix this and it will be OK
it will be OK it will be OK OK OK

I repeat this OK
over and over again

I try to be pragmatic
and rational, like you

I write a to-do list of things
that are sensible and practical

ways that I can help you heal
when you are allowed home

I google how to nurse you
but mostly I just

watch the door and
howl in the hallway

and pine
and whimper

the truth is
I'm a dog

I pace the house
and watch the door

soft padding of my paws
slippers on the wood floor

I whine and I
whimper and wait

watching, waiting
longing, listening

how can it be I'm at home
but so homesick?

you are my
home

I long for you
the sound of you

I listen for your key
turning in the lock

your footsteps in the hall
your hello hello hello voice

I sit on the stairs and watch the door
and wait and listen and

wait and listen
and wait.

Dirty Old Men

Teenagers are told they are too young to vote but
old enough to serve the desires of oligarchs and
dirty old men they are told they are too young to
be valid too young to be justified in their protest
and too young to buy booze too young to know
their own identity and to choose their love their sex
their gender their future and too young to demand
their freedom too young to choose their gods and
monsters and too young to protest but old enough
to flee war and cross continents and old enough to
wash up dead on beaches and old enough to be put
in cages at borders and old enough to be a child
bride and old enough to fend for themselves in
refugee camps and old enough to walk past and
ignore as they beg for change in a doorway and old
enough to be a soldier old enough to die in futile
wars for the profits of dirty old men teenagers are
too young to vote but old enough to be taken old
enough to be devoured too old to be acting so
innocent too young to be so big for their boots but
old enough to be the man of the house and old
enough to know they need to hide and run from
dirty old men teenagers are told they are too young
to vote too young to carry this burden of being

vilified and objectified by dirty old men who want
to eat them have them own them fuck them *Old
enough to bleed, old enough to breed* says the dirty old
man rubbing his knobbly vein greasing his loathe
with Vaseline slathering his throbbing entitlement
and his haemorrhoids and his purple bulbous ego
sores as a weeping mother in mourning makes good
morning telly use her floods of tears as lubricant
for dirty old men and teenagers are told they are
too young to vote too young to vote out the filth
too young to vote against dirty old men with their
dirty old man club and their dirty old man jokes
with their dirty old man bad breath with their
filthy outdated mentality dirty old men traditions
and dirty old men sucking cigars and dirty old men
falling asleep in the Houses of Parliament and
forever making the same pathetic excuses and
keeping the same handshakes and open secrets the
same slipping through loopholes of justice hiding
in plain sight hiding behind lies that dirty old men
have used for centuries as they eat the young with
their stale yellow teeth as they stamp on hope and
burn down love leaving disease and conflict on
tomorrow's doorstep for future teenagers to protest
who will also be told they are just teenagers and
too young to vote out the same dirty old men in a
stinking circle of dirty old men who are too old
and too sad and too mean see them scratching each
other's interests and investments with their filthy

fingernails caked in grotesque shit-flakes of corruption and greed and virus and death look at the dirty old man hands clawing at the young flesh of your sons and daughters on super-yachts and private jets and fingering the keyboards seeking: *hot teen loves it* see their guilty hands flecked with liver spots and stained with the blood of children who are never allowed to be safe to be children just being children just being teenagers.

One Hundred and Nine

I was one hundred and nine years old.
I was sitting on the end of my bed.
There was she, me, wild white hair, my
face with one hundred and nine years
of life. I saw my crooked yellow teeth
smile, oh no, much broader than a smile,
quite a wicked grin. And I lay there in
bed in shock, staring stupid. Me at Me.
The other me. The one hundred and
nine years old me, was sitting on the
bed, down by my feet and looking
straight back at me. She gave me such
a look as she turned and cocked her
head. She saw me awake in panic. She
saw how terribly worried I was. I was
so scared of her and so scared of the
dark and so scared of everything. Even
this. Even about meeting her who was
just me. This old me, aged one hundred
and nine years, with eyes so peculiar yet
so familiar, sage green, sea grey, old blue.
So calm and wry. Old moon face. Old
wise dog me. She started laughing at
me and my fear and my disbelief,

laughing at me clinging to my pillow. She laughed. Then she coughed, and she cleared her throat and then she said, 'Who taught you to fear you? Don't you get it yet? You're halfway forwards and halfway backwards, halfway there and halfway home. You are a little piece of everything old and everything new. You are sharing this evidence of love. There is no easy road. There are no templates. No guidelines. No maps. Not for the now, because there hasn't been a now before now. This is a mad man's world. And you'll never be mad enough. You'll never be rich enough. And you sure as hell ain't ever gonna be vicious enough. And so I ask you one question: how dare you be so afraid of yourself?'

Swans Are Hustlers

. . . she says, look at that swan, she is pointing with her pipe, look at that swan, that swan is lying to you, pretending to be so perfect and graceful, nobody can see how hard they kick underwater or how hard they work. They glide along, they make it look like they have it so easy. It's an illusion, you have to work hard to make such hard work look that easy. Think about it, everyone is struggling, paddling hard, pushing for work, pushing to get paid, pushing to get ahead and pushing to move forward, paddling hard to stay afloat. She lights and smokes her pipe, shakes her head slowly and then continues, you know, sometimes some people appear to glide, some people, they seem to glide through life, but it's all make-believe, the effort, the blood, sweat and tears, the intention drives you to keep going, it's the intention behind the work that keeps you awake at night, it a big fat lie that anything worthwhile is easy and effortless, she taps her pipe, exhales and stands to go and says, you're doing just fine, you just keep doing what you are doing, your generation, you young people, you're all doing great, you just gotta keep hustling, keep paddling, remember nothing good is easy or fast, and there is no such thing as gliding through life.

Malasana

I'm at London Bridge Tube
the Jubilee Line platform

there's a beautiful woman
with orange lips and long dark hair

she catches my attention
with her glorious blue-black hair

she smiles at me with tangerine lips
as we wait for the eastbound train

we stand side by side in the silence of the
empty train station, then she squats

right beside me, on the platform
I think she is crouching down to take a piss

I look down, and then I look away
then I look again, she has no underwear on

and I think she is photographing herself
in her reflection, in the glass wall

she has her phone in her hand
she is photographing her vagina

in her own reflection, it is intriguing
I try not to look, but it's very curious

I reason that she's probably . . .
just resting her legs

she is yoga squatting
she sits like a happy frog on a leaf

she's probably just yoga squatting
that's all, and I like the way she is doing that

resting on her haunches
I think it looks good

a malasana is a yoga squat
malasana is a good word

her hair is alive and black and
cascading down her back

her black skirt is gathered around her
she looks powerful and ancient

like she is washing clothes on a rock
and the train tracks are the river

she looks like she is cooking by open fire
stirring a pot of stew after the hunt

powerful goddess, squatting on her haunches
under the eternal stars and wild night

then the approaching train in the tunnel
becomes a tribal rhythm and a drum

as it thunders and rolls into the station
the train stops, the glass wall parts

and, as the doors open
she stands and brushes her skirt flat

turns and looks at me directly
and then she laughs and I laugh too

we laugh as we get into
the same empty train carriage

how we laugh and laugh
we both have a vagina

how funny it all is
how funny how

we are laughing
and how I remember

I also have a vagina
beneath my dress

my vagina her vagina
we both have a vagina

the train departs, the engine hums along
vagina-vagina vagina-vagina vagina-vagina

no, but she definitely photographed her vagina
was I in her photograph too? Did I look shocked?

I find it fascinating and odd and intriguing
and I am writing all of this in my phone

as the train moves I think about vaginas
her vagina and my vagina

and the train engine rhythm sings
vagina-vagina vagina-vagina vagina-vagina

she sits directly opposite me
I don't know where else to look

so we both stare down at our phone screens
sitting opposite each other in the empty carriage

she is writing in her phone
I am tapping this into my phone

she is writing something and it is as long
as this poem is taking to write

hang on? I am writing about her
do you think she is writing about me?

I doubt it, oh, hang on
she stopped typing and

I feel her looking at me
I have stopped typing too

I look up and she grins at me
pretty orange grin

long inky hair, she grins at me
slowly gathers her black skirt

I see her bare knees
pale thigh and skin as

she lifts her dress higher
I see bare legs and there she is

she is she is she is
she is smiling at me.

Sakura

we walk to the park
to see if our favourite
Japanese cherry tree
is in blossom yet
we hold hands
sharing joy in sakura
the first flowers are here
but the park is quite empty
we walk home again
strip in our hallway
put our outside clothes
on a hot wash
we wash our hands
bleach the doorknobs
sanitise our bolted door
we wash hands
we start on dinner
we make a Cullen Skink
and talk in the kitchen
I love you so much and
we're so lucky really
yes, we must count
our blessings
I love you too

yes we must
count our blessings
we just have
to be sensible
yes we must be
very careful
you wanna
peel potatoes?
OK, you say
first let me
wash my hands
I chop onions
wash my hands
I pull haddock
into chunks
and then
wash my hands
the radio is on
they talk about
washing hands
and wearing masks
and how to stay safe

I feel like
we're penguins
balancing an egg
on our feet
thin ice and snow
beneath our webbed feet
I feel like we're in a story
I ask you, do you remember
when the wind blows
I feel like
Raymond Briggs
wrote this year.

Kimono

Boxes of old dresses, kimonos, stage outfits and clothes: I sort through the armour I have worn. I remember being a little girl and watching my mother perform this very task; how she'd empty her old self onto the bed. Lay out her old wedding dress, her 1960s go-go boots, 1970s flower-power, hippy beads, sequins, glitter and wigs. She'd let me play dress up, tell me stories of other lives and the worlds before me, as she sorted through for things to donate to jumble sales or to repack with mothballs. There were dresses she'd save and keep nice and neat forever. But I'm alone right now, standing in front of my cloth shapes and these many costumes I have used.

See this, a crumbling and fragile white silk nightie. I wore it with German army boots, I wore it to mosh to Nirvana and Beastie Boys. I remember it now, this was the white nightie I wore when I fell down a well and lost my front tooth. Ah! And this is my favourite *Guitar Slut* T-shirt, this was what I was wearing in New York on the morning of 9/11 as the city exploded and the world was never the same, not after that day, and nor was I.

These are my turquoise cowboy boots. The heel so worn, the holes in the soles, a piece of cardboard inside. I wore these standing on pub tables doing poems for pints, staggering around festivals and the streets of the 1990s – Soho and Camden and Shoreditch. I also wore them to run. I wore them to protect myself from predators, to scarper from hotel rooms when it got weird, to walk home penniless at night with keys between my fingers. I love these boots I wore to be strong. I kicked ass in these.

This is the secondhand black pinstripe suit I wore at the BBC to smash the limitations of my being me. I held my own in this suit. And now looking back I realise I always made sure to dress up, to make an effort. A black and working-class upbringing teaches you to wear your best face.

I'll always hate this skirt. Please throw away the basic smart black pencil skirt. I don't know why I kept it. I remember I wore this at meetings and interviews. I tried so hard to sit up straight in that skirt, to be neat and tidy, to fit in – fuck trying so hard to fit in.

And look at this. This beautiful red taffeta dress, worn with a trilby, as I blazed my own trail. I booked my gigs, printed my own zines, recorded my work, explored the world like a wild poetry pirate . . . but I also remember how inside this red dress I could shrink, how I said sorry for saying sorry in this dress, *sorry sorry sorry*. I recall how I constantly put my hand in front of my mouth and said *sorry* in this dress and I wished for the courage that I have now. One day, you'll see how good it feels to be a bit older and you will learn to not say sorry and shrink to accommodate the comfort of others. One day you stop saying sorry for being you.

My favourite Vivienne Westwood dress. Electric-blue. It's got pockets. So sad to admit that when I wore it, other people's opinions clattered louder than my own better judgement. I couldn't see my own reflection, just what was projected onto me. I took so much bad advice in this perfect Westwood bodice. I put other people's opinions in the pockets. I should have told people to fuck off more when I was wearing Westwood. This vintage McQueen dress. It was a gift. My favourite lucky gig dress, both worn that first summer at the Edinburgh Fringe. The good old days of raving in the Port O' Leith and singing in the graveyard at dawn and living on nothing but a dream.

These are the clothes I wore to run away from myself. These are the clothes I wore to run to myself. I wanted to live, that's all, live — a thing which seemed so natural and easy for others — but to live, I mean to live well, I remember that felt like a big ask. For so many years I seemed to wear this invisible scarf knitted with melodrama and weaved with death wishes.

I don't know why I kept these all these objects. Maybe so I would remember to write about them and pass some of this courage on to you. Maybe so you will know better than I did, go further than I could. Maybe so you know I get it, I really do. We were always patted on the head and shushed, we were labelled and boxed, we were patronised and wholly underestimated.

I was once a young girl screaming FIRE and I hear you scream FIRE now.

These are the costumes I wore to fail and fall but get up again. Here is the armour I wore to try, try, try again. This my threadbare moth-eaten fur coat of failure, the ripped lining stuffed with self-sabotage. But here are the striped socks I pulled up, and here the camouflage I stopped wearing. And here's a beautiful silk kaftan, the pattern of healing amethyst, the pockets filled with the desire to be more faithful and more gentle with myself.

And I write this today because I want you to have an easier time than I did. I want you to be more patient and more kind to yourself. It took such a long time to write a page like this, but here it is. I hope you recognise yourself somewhere in here, my love, I hope you hear me and I hope I do you justice.

Here is my favourite yellow kimono, here my silver boots, see, this is one of the superhero costumes that I save myself in.

Now it is time for you to get up, get dressed and save yourself.

City of Water

My Italian friend
Gigi once said:
Beware when
Venice floods,
because when
Venice floods
it's the beginning
of the end of the world.

I remember his
words of warning
and watch the news.
It feels like the
beginning of the end
of the world, Gigi.
Brown floodwater
and rising tides here,
and raging fires and
black smoke there.
Everywhere is chaos,
the migration of people
losing their homes,
all over the planet
we are unsettled.

Today Venice is flooded.
Venice is under water.
Tomorrow who knows?
I want to speak to Gigi now –
I know if he were alive
he'd be so crazy and he'd
be on the phone yelling,
with his incredible energy
and passion for humanity.
He'd be swearing, chain-smoking,
trying to raise funds for Venice.

I'm sad I never went to Venice,
I have never seen the city of water,
never stolen a kiss under a bridge,
or held hands in a moonlit gondola.

But when we gathered
at Gigi's funeral I felt it –
there is so much world to see,
so much wonder to share and
so much life to fight for.

And the Moon Don't
Talk to Me Anymore

and starlings swing on a skeleton in a
cage, pecking at the fat and the meat
and the seed

the cherry blossom, pink and plastic,
bought for a fiver from Chinatown

and the moon don't talk to me anymore

and my white tablecloth is stained with
coffee, which came from a country
already in flames

and the moon don't talk to me anymore

she is rising fat and full and furious
with grief, a mourning that washes
up tide after tide that rises with the
moon tonight, the salt water crashing
to shore

and the moon don't talk to me anymore

and the night is dead, and the dark is long, and the rain pours down like the sky's all a river, and the moon don't sing, and the moon won't sing, and the fear spreads and rises and seeps into everything, like a bad smell or like smoke under your door

and the moon don't talk to me anymore

and you have memories of sleeping in your clothes, like a dog on a blanket on the floor — are these memories or premonitions from now or prewar?

and the moon don't talk to me anymore

and the earth hangs heavy, and the sun has turned his back and all I see is his coat of clouds, and the rain washes decency away, kindness is a closed charity shop, but the sound of the washing machine is a comfort, it's like the sound of the sea from what you remember, from a postcard someone sent you from before, remember? It was stuck to your fridge door, it said *I wish you were here*, and I do, I wish you were here

and the moon don't talk to me anymore

but a full fridge feels safe, and so we
stock up the store, they say it's safest to
get a delivery, and we buzz on the
internet like bees, oh, we are the lucky
ones, aren't we, hiding at home, locked
in our houses, wearing pyjamas, boosting
the heating, try not to think of the poor
or the elderly, those that aren't safe and
those that aren't eating, think of the
food banks and the people in cages, and
the kids that need that one hot school
meal, suddenly, it gets real, and think
of all the folk who cannot afford the
bills, the unpaid time off work, medi-
cine and pills, your heart keeps the score

and the moon don't talk to me anymore

now her milky face seems clotted with
uncertainty, and the gods are all stone-
cold silent today, and the blue sky is a
box-set you binge, hope is at the bottom
of a well, there's a hole in my bucket
but I keep turning the handle

and the moon don't talk to you anymore
and the moon don't talk to me anymore

I hum along to an empty fridge, I talk
to the washing machine, because its face
is as round as the moon, like a dog, I
sleep on the floor

and the moon don't talk to me anymore

Cake

Take one rainy Sunday afternoon. Add a pinch of radio. Lie on the sofa. Listen to the rain. Read a beautiful book and drink tea. When tea is perfect sipping temperature, you may find you have a need for cake. You have to REALLY need cake or this won't work. It is an emergency. Remember you need cake. Quite urgently. This will give you the motivation to make yourself a cake. Go to the kitchen with nothing but cake-hunger and a compelling intention to make cake. Hang on! Maybe you should make a gin and tonic first. Tastes good. A perfect gin and tonic. Now! Mission! Cake! Put the oven on. Put music on and dance a bit. Sip some gin. Nice. Get a big bowl. Stir dry ingredients with big wooden spoon: polenta, flour, desiccated coconut, ground almond, baking powder, pinch of salt. You make it up as you go along, sing along to the radio and sip gin. You are gonna make a cake. Nothing gonna stop you now. Look at you go! Now add some grease: maybe some butter or maybe some coconut oil. Maybe a spoon of one and a fork of the other. Play it by ear and keep tasting it as you go and feeling the cake energy coming together. Add caster sugar, I guess, maybe about four spoons. Rub it all together like you are making apple crumble. Now wet stuff: Let's add a cap of vanilla essence. Give a tin of coconut milk a really good shake and add half the tin. Stir together with dry ingredients, it's got good cake vibes now. In a separate bowl whisk one egg and then fold it in slowly. I have no idea if you even need this egg. But it is important to take a moment here to have a happy memory of baking cakes and of ingredients being folded in very slowly, so you fold the egg in slowly. Fold in that happy feeling. And while you do it: daydream. Remember your childhood. Recall a distant time, being so small and standing on a chair, you as a little person watching and waiting to lick the bowl. Ah, now feel that love. Love for the then and the here and now. You are past and present in the cake. Tear a handful of fresh raspberries into pieces and add. Put the rest of the raspberries to the side. You need them for decoration and the icing too. Add cranberries and raspberries through your cake mixture. The cranberries I used were those dried Craisins left over from Christmas. Add a handful of flaked almonds. It looks like a golden summer meadow littered with poppies. Your mixture is buttery yellow with raspberry swirls, it should look a bit like melted raspberry ripple ice-cream and it smells amazing. Now add a shot of rum. Then add a squeeze of lemon for luck. Taste it. Is it sweet enough? Tart enough? Coconutty enough? Add more coconut. Possibly more coconut. Yeah more coconut. You love coconut. You want it to be like a Bakewell tart and a lemon polenta cake had a baby. Get a cake tin. Grease it with a knob of butter. Hang on! Take a moment to be surprised you own a cake tin. Well done you. Now, swirl desiccated coconut around the inside of the tin so it will stick to the butter and coat the outside of the cake with toasted coconut when its cooked.

Good thinking. Suddenly you are like some kinda cake wizard. Now pour mixture into cake tin. Bake for 30 minutes. At some point your lover or flatmate or a family member will probably enter the kitchen. Please act cool. Act like you know what you are doing. Act like you make cakes all the time. Maybe make sure you have put an apron on or throw the tea towel over your shoulder all knowing and nonchalant. Don't get sidetracked or explain your messy cake methods or it will break the spell. Now to make a topping. You need another big bowl and a wooden spoon. Pour remainder of coconut milk into bowl. Maybe add some double cream. Lick spoon. You are the cat that got the cream. Maybe add a bit of butter to mixture. And then some icing sugar. Add some desiccated coconut. More icing sugar. Beat it, whip it, beat it, whip it. Until it is peaky and stiff. Beat raspberries into it. Now the icing or butter cream or whatever this is called, look at it, it is turning pink! PINK! You made it pink! I am so proud of you. Keep tasting it. You want it to taste a bit coconutty and almondy. But also tart and lush from the fresh raspberries. Keep tasting it until it is as creamy, fruity, sweet and coconutty as you like. Dance and sip your gin and wash up the bowls. Clean up all that mess you made so far, spillages and scattered coconut sprinkles. Check cake. Cake isn't cooking! Ah, no! Put it back in for another 10 minutes. Maybe bake for about 45 minutes. So that's 30 – then check it – then put it back in for another 15, OK? Maybe? Kitchen smells really, really good.

Make another gin and tonic. Your lover or friend or family member will come in and want to help, let them whip your topping hard. With big strong arms. This is not a euphemism but your topping is really stiff now. Check the oven. Cake is cooked! Wow, it worked! Say HOORAY! Put cake in fridge to cool. Toast some desiccated coconut and flaked almonds. Add a pinch of brown sugar. Leave to cool. Do an excited dance. Go out to garden and say: Guess what — I made cake! Your love is waving at you, all gorgeous and muddy. The tomatoes are flowering and the rain has stopped. The world smells beautiful after the rain. You feel very lucky. Go back inside. Decorate the cake with a flat spatula. Smear the whole cake with pink icing mixture. Spin it, rotate it. You are a sculptor now so sculpt the cake. Go smooth around the sides. Scatter with the toasted coconut and almonds. Decorate with last of the fresh raspberries. Finish with a dusting of icing sugar. Instagram it. It is very rare you make cake. You did what? Made a cake! Piece of cake! Have your cake and eat it! Go back to your sofa. Sigh lovingly at your Sunday accomplishments. Your pile of brilliant and beautiful books and your tea and your slice of cake. Today your life is simple. You are a lucky thing. You are blessed. You are loved.

You made cake.

First Mother

I am rebel soul
warrior, healer
old blood.

I read my DNA results,
I retraced my roots:
I come from before,
snow and oceans,
jungle and sand,
stars and fire.

I'm naturally
drawn to water
to salt and flame,
we will gather to
warm our bones
like we always did.

I can picture the first mother
kneading bread by a fire
with big strong hands,
how she has kneaded me
into this human shape
of life and spirit.

First mother,
she who baked bread
in an imagined village
in ancient lands
of long ago.

And by that roaring fire
once upon a time,
she cooked for us all.
I can close my eyes and
see her, both hands gripping
the spoon to stir the pot,
steam and hiss and heat,
the beat of her swaying breasts,
her shuddering hips,
her redemption song.

She was our survival.
She was all weather
and moonshine,
all sea, salt and oil
and flame and water.

We are nothing but
she, reincarnated
cycles and circles,
she comes around
eternal, endurance.

And the first snow
is her reminder,
she is tapping softly
at my window,
and the sunrise
is gold in my eyes,
triggering visions
of past lives.

A Small Kindness

Forgive yourself
you forget to
forgive yourself
you were in danger
forgive yourself
you believed a lie
forgive yourself
it went too far
forgive yourself
the broken glass
forgive yourself
you're forgiving them
forgive yourself
you blame yourself
forgive yourself
you got hurt
forgive yourself
you got lost
forgive yourself
you were you
forgive yourself
for not forgiving yourself
forgive yourself
forgive yourself.

Great-Granddaughters

We are the granddaughters of the witches they couldn't burn.

Maybe some of you. But let's be honest, many of you are the great-granddaughters of a lady in a house, and maybe, she was protected by title and wealth, husband and church. And so to be more truthful, or at least historically correct, that great-grandmother of yours did a lot of praying and needlework and had servants and slaves and privilege, as the patriarchy spread fear and hate and pointed WITCH to a penniless, wild-haired woman a bit like my great-grandmothers, who were not dangerous witches, but more like healers or medicine women, who were living in the mountains and rainforest, just gazing at the stars, talking to the full moon and making tea for their period pain from ganja leaf.

I Cannot Wait to Breathe

I cannot wait, I cannot wait, I cannot wait
until we can talk about all of this in the past tense
I cannot wait for these to be the old days
I cannot wait for that, I cannot wait for tomorrow
I cannot wait for it unravel and come apart
I cannot wait to see how the truth will surface
and how we will learn how deep the rot went
I cannot wait to be in my pyjamas on my sofa
watching the documentary of this time on TV
see how they all got caught and arrested
how they grassed each other up in the end
how the bank and phone records will tell the story
and how the shaking phone footage will be shocking
but look so grainy and outdated to our future selves
and our clothes and shoes will be of another time
and our architecture and cars so old-timey and strange
and how the movie of this scandal will be an epic film
about how it all worked out OK in the end
because it will all be OK in the end, won't it?
see how the court cases were televised
how it was a spectacular example of justice
how the judge who sent them down
was a powerful black woman

how the bastards never got away with any of it in the end
I cannot wait for the end of this, I cannot wait
I cannot wait to talk about all of this in the past tense
to say, yeah, that was then, this is now
see how we learned so much

I cannot wait, I cannot wait, I cannot wait
I cannot wait to live in a tomorrow world
when the struggle is over and the work is finished
when it is all about recovery, when the worry is done
when we don't have to worry like this
every day . . . not anymore
imagine not feeling . . . like . . . this . . . all the time
I cannot wait, I cannot wait for the new day
when a question in the pub quiz could be:
In what year did we smash the patriarchy?
Imagine how good those first cold beers will taste
how happy we will all be to be together again
a room filled with excited chatter and laughter
how there will be music, oh, how we will dance
and we'll watch the sun rise together again
how we will breathe in that new morning
how we will breathe in that new morning
how we will breathe in that new morning
as we have never been permitted to breathe before.

Your Fears Are Not Prophecies

These fears that are huge
in your head right now,
the loops of words and
unhelpful thoughts,
that are making you
anxious and unhappy,
they are not premonitions
of what is gonna happen,
they are stories and memories,
they are not prophecies
of what happens next –
who knows what happens next?
Nobody knows.
So sit with this page now
take a deep breath
give time a chance
make some room
make some space
so that something
truly miraculous
can happen
next.

2084

After George Orwell's 1984

PART ONE

Ext. / Narrator / Poet

It's a bright cold day in June and the clock remains silent. My chin nuzzles into my scarf in an effort to shield my face from the surveillance camera above the dusty glass doors of the Old Word Bank. Inside, the hallway smells of burnt books, there are ashy pages underfoot. A large framed poster is nailed to the wall. It depicts The Word Bill: the list of the new rules and directives written in the mouth of the flat-faced man with pink-ham-coloured features. I've been told to collect my paperwork from the Poetry Office. I climb the stairs, anxious that I may be too late and that my paperwork may have already been incinerated.

The door to the Poetry Office is ajar, and I push it open tentatively. I find the room ransacked, whoever came before me has destroyed every trace of poetry. With my heart pounding, I turn on my heels and hurry down the fire escape. Once outside I try to catch my breath. Then a wordless beggar approaches me with a sign: *small words, small words, Big Issue?* and it is then, as I go to reach for my dictionary to give him some spare verbs, that six armed Word Enforcement Officers approach me. There's nowhere to run. They handcuff me and lead me away. I brace myself for the silent torture of the detention centre known to all poets as Word Prison.

PART TWO

The Word Prison, an interrogation room, where our poet has been cross-examined for many hours. Silent now, but for the rustle of paper, a jangle of keys.

Officer: Please use only the plain words as permitted in accordance with the Word Bill. No fancy talk. No poetic speak. No frilly language. No pretty double meanings. No underlying messages. No depth of feeling. No emotion. No empathic phrasing. No romantic gestures. No comedic interludes. No jokes. No foul language. No blasphemy. No displays of emotion and manipulation. No dramatic pauses. No theatrics. No foreign words. No soliloquies. No limericks. No monologues. No sonnets. No rhyming couplets. No sestina. No poetics in any shape or form.

    We ask you one more time: What were you doing at the Old Word Bank?

Poet: Listen, I don't know why I'm in here, I told you this already. I am a fully paid up union member,

I registered to write new poems, all my paperwork is legal — I mean, I haven't actually got my paperwork to hand, but . . .

Officer: Answer in 140 characters or less only, please. Why were you at the Old Word Bank?

Poet: I was told to go to the Poetry Office. They had said they'd look after my words for me, that my words could earn a high interest and as long as I paid my union fees, I was free to write poems and dream big dreams . . .

Officer: May I remind you of the law: the office knows who has the rights to poetry and ideas and dreams and the Word Enforcement Office are by law obliged to obtain all information about all poems. Are you aware of this law? You are? For the purposes of the recording the detainee is nodding.

Poet: But, but . . . these so-called laws are corrupt, they are only in place to make profits for those that control poetry and the hidden meanings in words and . . .

Officer: Please just answer the question. How did you gain access to the Old Word Bank? Who were you meeting there?

Poet: I received a message from the office to go there,
            I have . . .

Officer   You were sent a message, yes, who sent you this
            message? Where is it?

Poet: I . . .

Officer: Simply answer yes or no: are you aware that all
            poetry should be sourced and shared legitimately?
            Are you aware that poems are not to be plundered
            from restricted zones and sourced from black-
            market dreams and illegal visions? Do you know
            the law? Have you read and signed the Word Bill?
            Simply answer yes or no?

Poet: Yes. But . . .

Officer: Then can you explain these? I am showing detainee
            classified object 123A and object 123B. Are these
            your dictionary and thesaurus? And here, object
            123C − an illegally obtained library card? Is this
            yours? And object 123D − I believe this is your
            diary and here, object 123E, a handwritten notebook?

Poet: I don't understand. Yes, they are. They've been
            certified. That's an old government-issue thesaurus,
            it's vintage, my grandmother gave it to me when
            she was . . .

Officer: So for the last time, is this your poetry? Did you write your dreams down in these notebooks? We are here to fight the scourge of word evasion, we are here to expose poets and rascals, dreamers and libertines. We'll have your tongue for this.

Poet: Word evasion? No way! I was just dreaming. It's one law for us, and another for you. I pay the union for my right to write, my poems are locally sourced, my dreams are mined from my own mind and I declared every exclamation mark!

Officer: I'm arresting you for being complicit in aggressive dreaming and word evasion, with coercion to share your words, for aiding and abetting illegal poetic thoughts. You will be charged with suspicion of word profiteering by way of placing your poetry for free into online offshore social media accounts. You have incited poetry! You have the right to remain silenced. Any words you say now can and will be used against you in a court of law. You have the right to speak words to an attorney, and must have an attorney present during any further use of words. Take her downstairs, Sergeant, have her books burnt and her language labelled.

PART THREE

Solitary confinement, a hollow-sounding prison cell

Int. / Narrator / Poet:

If you want to keep a secret,
you must hide it from yourself,
locked in solitary silence.
This I tell myself.
That once upon a poem,
in this town called nowadays,
where bracken grew,
and smog was thick
and truths were so few,
where concrete and daydream
tangled in wire like spaghetti
between the roots of all evil,
spoiling the view.
Where the rivers gurgled brown,
the sewage all-churning,
where city banks shone gold
with the money they were earning,
where the game seemed the same
but the worm was always turning,
and the holes in their pockets were
from the promises burning.

This was where a lie
was born to be king,
and with each new untruth
it tore through everything,
silence scorched the tongue
and burnt all work hours,
the midwife cut the umbilical cord
and ink came out in showers,
and the sounds of all words
oozed out, indigo blue,
a system not for the many
but just for the few.
Dreams banked and hidden
in a bottomless inkwell,
as long as the hoarders got fatter
nobody would tell.
The silence was stifling,
the greed, so loud, so clever,
but the urge to share words
was still as strong as ever.

Speaking up, we got somewhere,
our courage was so bold,
for a poet never can unlearn
a poem we're told, unsee a story unfold.
When there are not enough words left,
when the letters all run dry,
we pay back, to pay back,
a truth hid in a lie.

See your protestors are children,
and the unheard all cry,
the libraries got closed down
and we're all gonna fry,
the damage is brutal,
don't turn a blind eye,
don't leave the sick and
the weak to suffer and die.
Now your babies are soldiers,
your hospitals shuttered,
the sick and the weak,
the displaced in the gutters.
You bleed all the words dry
until nothing survives,
we're holding on to each other
for our dear lives,
grabbing for life rafts,
grabbing at stale crumbs,
grabbed by the throat
we are dumbed and numbed —
fear is dead air
and silence is a gun,
united we must sing,
singing as one.

It's a startling thing,
a destruction of the unsaid,
we meet in a dark place
where books are found dead.

The consequence of corruption,
well, that's nothing new,
ignorance is bliss,
and who needs to know, knew.
It's a terrifying thing,
the dissolving of choices,
shushing and muting and
killing your voices.
In a time of apathy,
hope is a revolutionary act,
weaving fearless love
into fiction and fact.

Wonderful World

The day I show my mother the internet for the first time she's cautious about it. This is Google Earth, I tell her. She thinks it's a picture, she thinks it is a game. I show her the spinning blue ball. This is us, this is us on planet Earth. I try to explain. Look! I type in Jamaica. Look! We find Bull Head Mountain, her fingertips on a blue spinning ball. Her face lights up as we zoom in, she shows me to her school, the family home, the places where she was a girl in the long-ago now in the present. Then I open YouTube and ask, What do you want to see? Pick anything, Mum, literally anything! Look at this funny cat video! Watch this dance! What do you want to see? She is baffled. I don't know, she says quietly, Do they have Louis Armstrong? Can it show me Louis Armstrong? I watch Mum's face watching Louis Armstrong singing, his grainy black and white image flickering on the screen, I see her face soften and smile, as he sings, *I see trees of green, red roses too, I see them bloom, for me and you.* Her eyes are shining and I hug her. I think we could all do with more Louis Armstrong, his wonderful world right there in the palm of our hands.

Dry Land

It is a bit like being
set adrift in a small boat
not sturdy enough
for such an arduous journey.

We hold hands as we lose sight
of land and all we know, we hold
on to the boat, to each other, to hope,
and by some miracle we weather the first squall.

You are stronger
than you know, you must be.
This boat is made of love, love, love,
but the news hits us like a tsunami.

Suddenly,
we are in a strange scene,
told to sit quietly at a table
and to listen to some words.

Each word alarming
thunder and lightning
and in that moment
a rope snaps and we lose it.

Our boat is thrown
in violent dark water.
The winter is harsh,
adrift in chemotherapy.

We are swallowed in
rogue waves of fear and uncertainty,
the operations, the procedures
send us overboard into icy water.

We cling to scraps of news like driftwood,
as giant sea monsters rise from the unknown.
They see our feet kicking above their
sharp teeth and hunger below.

Then we are becalmed
on a frozen sea, frozen fog,
nothing to see, frozen sea, frozen fog,
time stops, we wait, hold our breath, wait.

A strange contradiction
of needing to talk about it
and not wanting to talk about it —
the words a language I don't know.

And the only person
I want to talk to is you.
I want to talk about
my love to my love.

Paddling with numb hands,
exhausted, treading water,
pray for warmth, pray for time,
pray for a soft summer and dry land.

Is it safe
to breathe yet?
No. Salt water fills the lungs
and stings your red eyes.

Another
violent morning.
We are hit with another deluge,
our boat rocking wildly off course,

hard rain slashing down, relentless
I feel so hopeless and stupid.
It feels like I'm scooping water out
of a paper boat with a tea cup.

I am not
very good at this,
I haven't
done it before.

The rough sea
swallows us whole.
I see blood and my love
drowning in waves of pain.

A doctor yanks him
back on board
a shark stalks us, circling,
knocking at the bow.

There's a hole in the hold,
hold my hand and don't let go,
and don't ever let go and
never leave me. OK.

As I write this it is all still —
a gentle sun, the first of spring.
So grateful for calm waters today.
Above us seabirds swoop in blue skies,

and we count blessings
thankful for the good weather,
lucky that we made it to this point.
Say it again: We are so lucky.

I mend our torn sails
with an eye fixed on the horizon
I prayed for summer and dry land.
My love sits in the sun and eats a tangerine.

With Love, Grief and Fury 5

Spring 2024

with love, grief and fury
my eyes blurred with tears
I cannot write this page

everywhere, chaos, conflict
the global mourning
can be seen from space

trust your grief
it is trying to
show you the truth

believe your tears
they are crying to
show you your strength

Acknowledgements

'And You Will Go' was the first of the very new poems I shared from this book – with thanks to Green Gathering, Writers Mosaic, the British Library, Hastings Book Festival and Apples and Snakes, QEH, at the Southbank Centre. 'The Girl in the Green Cardigan' is dedicated to Elif Shafak who invited me to speak at Literature Beyond Borders, a Choose Love charity event for the people of Syria and Turkey. 'My Heart Is a Boat' was performed at the Royal Albert Hall for Windrush 75, a stellar event curated by Trevor Nelson and broadcast on BBC Radio 2. This poem began life titled 'No Holds Barred' and was published by Tangerine Press and Rough Trade Books. Earlier versions of 'Cathedrals' and 'Blackbird' were published in *Fishing in the Aftermath* by Burning Eye Books. Another version of 'Laughing by the Toaster' titled 'Love and Laughter' was shortlisted in the Bridport Poetry Prize. The first draft of 'Bees' was performed at the Roundhouse, Camden, accompanied by grime violinist Tanya Cracknell, as part of HUH curated by composer Jasmin Kent Rodgman. Sections of '2084' were used in a BBC commission *From Fact to Fiction* with poet Kate Fox for Radio 4. 'And the Moon Don't Talk To Me Anymore' was created during lockdown; accompanied by music by composer Anna Phoebe, this lockdown collaboration was performed and filmed remotely and then shared at York Cathedral as part of York Festival. A version of 'City of Water' was published in an anthology of climate fiction titled *Sunburnt Saints* by Seventy2One. 'I Want To Be Your Wife' and 'Sun Cream in February' featured on *The Lockdown E.P.* released by Nymphs & Thugs during the lockdowns, with half of all sales donated to NHS charities. These two poems have been shared and performed at various festivals and events, including Out-Spoken at the Purcell Room, Southbank, Tongue Fu at the Arnolfini in Bristol, and Nymphs & Thugs' LIVEwire. You can find an 'I Want to Be Your Wife' poetry-film made by Idle Work Factory on YouTube; recently that poetry-film was selected by artist Sarah Lucas for the *Big Women* exhibition at First Site, Colchester in May 2023.

'Five Words' is dedicated to Sarah Everard, Bibaa Henry and Nicole Smallman and to all who just wish to just walk home in peace. 'I Will Walk You Home' is dedicated to poet Gboyega Odubanjo.

Thank you to all bookshops, booksellers and libraries, to all event organisers and festivals, supporters, readers and writers, students and teachers, to my beautiful friends, supreme poets and artists and storytellers who inspire me to read and write and learn something new every day. Thank you to all of my family, my siblings, thanks to my lovely mum. Special thank you to Dickie for laughing by the toaster with me for all these years, for always and for everything.

With love and thanks to

Agent	Crystal Mahey-Morgan
Editor and copy-editor	Martha Sprackland
Commissioning Editor	Leah Woodburn
Head of Editorial Management	Vicki Rutherford
Managing Editor	Leila Cruickshank
Proofreader	Edward Crossan
Typesetter	Palimpsest Book Production
Head of Publicity	Lucy Zhou
Deputy Marketing Director	Caitriona Horne
Cover Design	Valeri Rangelov
Rights and Contracts Director	Jessica Neale
Senior Rights Manager	Charlie Tooke
Rights Executive	Phyllis Armstrong
Head of Production	Kate Oliver
Sales Director	Joanna Lord
Head of International Sales	Stephanie Scott
Head of UK Sales	Sasha Cox
Audio and Digital Manager	Gaia Poggiogalli
Publisher	Jamie Byng

Last Words

So many of the writers and artists we love create work in the trenches of war and brutality, hunger and heartache. Their love, grief and fury echo and resonate now more than ever. This trauma is timeless. Read the lyrics. Hear the notes. Feel the rhythm. Your old vinyl and books are rooted in the truth of the struggle, just think of the original blues and jazz rebels and the first hope punks. The artist you wear on your t-shirt was born of resistance. How they sang. How they marched for civil liberties and human rights, how they spoke out against war and for the health of our planet. For love and peace. For equality, emancipation and justice. See how they wove their love, grief and fury into the materials of the world. So much of the art we treasure is vibrating with protest. It is made out of the truth of us. It warns us that the future is now and that now is all we have.

As this book goes to print I leave you with a salute and solidarity, an offering of blank pages for you, the reader. I wish us to unite in this last words ritual and I hope that you write from your own heart, share your words of love and grief and fury. You might write a poem or prayer, a memory or dream of a person that came to your mind as you read these poems. As the years pass, if this book is borrowed or passed along, these names, your words and hopes, your love, grief and fury will live on. As you finish this book, pick up a pen, write the names of love, someone you celebrate, something you truly cherish. These pages are left blank for you to mark this grief, this timeless and universal mourning, our humanity and spirit, fire and fury. United we share in these last words and healing pages in acknowledgement of all we fear, all we love and are loving, for all we lost and are losing, and for all we fight for.

Your expressions of love, grief and fury are valuable. We need each other now more than ever. Hold the line. Share your courage. Rally against tides of apathy and despondency. Be witness. Be present. Write the tomorrow you wish to see. Picture it. Vocalise it. Visualise it. Write it. Sing it. As Nina Simone once said, *I'll tell you what freedom is to me: no fear.* What is freedom to you? Can you look her in the eye and hold her gaze and show her how she is found?